A Devoted Son
and other
Indian Short Stories

Annotations and Additional Materials
by Noreen O'Donovan

Ernst Klett Sprachen
Stuttgart

A Devoted Son and other Indian Short Stories

Worterklärungen und zusätzliche Materialien von
Noreen O'Donovan, Pforzheim

1. Auflage 1 8 7 6 5 4 | 2018 17 16 15

Alle Drucke dieser Auflage sind unverändert und können im Unterricht nebeneinander verwendet werden. Die letzte Zahl bezeichnet das Jahr dieses Druckes.

Internetadresse: www.klett-sprachen.de

Redaktion: Rona McGeoch; Gabriele Uplawski, Redaktionsbüro Hannover
Umschlagfoto: Shutterstock Images /© Semenev Gleb
Druck: CEWE Stiftung & KGaA, Germering
Printed in Germany

ISBN 978-3-12-577514-5

9 783125 775145

Contents

Abbreviations

The following abbreviations are used in the annotations in this book:

AE	American English
BE	British English
b.	born
derog	derogative
e.g.	exempli gratia; for example
esp.	especially
etc.	et cetera
fig	figurative
form	formal
i.e.	id est; that is
Ind.E	Indian English
inf	informal
l.	line
opp.	opposite
os	oneself
p. /pp.	page/pages
pl	plural
sb	somebody
sth	something
usu	usually
vulg	vulgar

Anita Desai

About the Author

Anita Desai was born Anita Mazumdar, the daughter of a Bengali businessman and a mother of German origin, in 1937. She grew up in Mussoorie, a hill station north of Delhi. Though her first language was German, she began to write in English at the age of seven, and published her first stories two years later.

After secondary school in Delhi, she studied at Delhi University, where she received a B.A. in English Literature in 1957. In the following year she married businessman Ashvin Desai; they have four children.

Anita Desai's first novel, *The Peacock* was published in Britain in 1963. Several of her subsequent novels were not only popular successes, but winners of important literary awards: *Fire on the Mountain* (1977), for example, won her both the National Academy of Letters Award and the Winifred Holtby Memorial prize. For *The Village by the Sea* (1982), she was awarded the Guardian Children's Fiction Prize. She was short-listed three times for the prestigious Booker Prize – in 1980 for *The Clear Light of Day*, in 1984 for *In Custody* (which was later turned into a Merchant-Ivory film), and in 1999 for *Fasting, Feasting*.

Between these major works, she continued to write short stories, and published several collections. "A Devoted Son" was first published in *Games at Twilight* (1982), and also chosen for inclusion in *The Penguin Book of Indian Short Stories* (1991).

The characters in Anita Desai's stories and novels tend to be members of the Anglicized Indian middle class, with their personal and marital problems in the forefront. Though she does not claim to write overtly political stories, her works do indirectly reflect the realities of Indian society. *The Clear Light of Day*, for example, is set in 1947, and told against the background of a country in which Hindus and Muslims are torn apart by partition into the two separate states of India and Pakistan. In *Baumgartner's Bombay* (1988), she uses her own half-German background to view the poverty-stricken city through the eyes of a Jewish refugee forced to live among them, taking care of stray cats.

Having lived in various Indian cities, Anita Desai moved with her daughter Kiran (see pp. 80–84) to England to take up an invitation to teach at Cambridge University. She finally separated from her husband, and never returned permanently to India. She now lives mainly in the United States, where she is Professor of Writing at Massachussetts Institute of Technology (MIT). She is a Fellow of the Royal Society of Literature, and a member of the American Academy of Arts and Letters.

Anita Desai

A Devoted Son

When the results appeared in the morning papers, Rakesh scanned them, barefoot and in his pyjamas, at the garden gate, then went up the steps to the verandah where his father sat sipping his morning tea and bowed down to touch his feet.

'A first division, son?' his father asked, beaming, reaching for the papers.

'At the top of the list, papa,' Rakesh murmured, as if awed. 'First in the country.'

Bedlam broke loose then. The family whooped and danced. The whole day long visitors streamed into the small yellow house at the end of the road, to congratulate the parents of this Wunderkind, to slap Rakesh on the back and fill the house and garden with the sounds and colours of a festival. There were garlands and halwa, party clothes and gifts (enough fountain pens to last years, even a watch or two), nerves and temper and joy, all in a multicoloured whirl of pride and great shining vistas newly opened: Rakesh was the first son in the family to receive an education, so much had been sacrificed in order to send him to school and then medical college, and at last the fruits of their sacrifice had arrived, golden and glorious.

To everyone who came to him to say, 'Mubarak, Varmaji, your son has brought you glory,' the father said, 'Yes, and do you know what is the first thing he did when he saw the results this morning? He came and touched my feet. He bowed down and touched my feet.' This moved many of the women in the crowd so much that they were seen to raise the ends of their saris and dab at their tears while the men reached out for the betel-leaves and sweetmeats that were offered around on trays and shook their heads in wonder and approval of such exemplary filial

devoted feeling or showing great loyalty – 5 **first division** *here:* highest category of marks – 5 **to beam** to smile broadly – 7 **to awe** to cause great wonder and respect – 9 **bedlam** noisy chaos and confusion (from the name of a famous London 'madhouse') – 9 **to whoop** to make loud, joyous cries – 14 **garland** woven string of flowers – 14 **halwa** a sweet dish made of semolina (*Weizengrieß*), nuts and spices – 16 **whirl** (*here fig*) continuous circular movement – 16 **vista** wide view (*here:* of future possibilities) – 18 **to sacrifice** to give up, do without (for a higher reason) – 27 **to dab** to wipe dry – 27 **betel** ['bi:təl] plant that produces nuts and leaves with a mildly narcotic effect – 28 **sweetmeat** cake, dessert, or other sweet dish – 29 **filial** appropriate to a son behaviour. 'One does not often see such behaviour in sons any more,' they all agreed, a little enviously perhaps. Leaving the house, some of the women said, sniffing, 'At least on such an occasion they might have served pure ghee sweets,' and some of the men said, 'Don't you think old Varma was giving himself airs? He needn't think we don't remember that he comes from the vegetable market himself, his father used to sell vegetables, and he has never seen the inside of a school.' But there was more envy than rancour in their voices and it was, of course, inevitable – not every son in that shabby little colony at the edge of the city was destined to shine as Rakesh shone, and who knew that better than the parents themselves?

And that was only the beginning, the first step in a great, sweeping ascent to the radiant heights of fame and fortune. The thesis he wrote for his M. D. brought Rakesh still greater glory, if only in select medical circles. He won a scholarship. He went to the USA (that was what his father learnt to call it and taught the whole family to say – not America, which was what the ignorant neighbours called it, but, with a grand familiarity, "the USA") where he pursued his career in the most prestigious of all hospitals and won encomiums from his American colleagues which were relayed to his admiring and glowing family. What was more, he came back, he actually returned to that small yellow house in the once-new but increasingly shabby colony, right at the end of the road where the rubbish vans tipped out their stinking contents for pigs to nose in and rag-pickers to build their shacks on, all steaming and smoking just outside the neat wire fences and well-tended gardens. To this Rakesh returned and the first thing he did on entering the house was to slip out of the embraces of his sisters and brothers and bow down and touch his father's feet.

3 **to sniff** to breathe sharply (*here:* as an expression of disapproval) – 4 **ghee** clarified butter (used a lot in Indian cooking) – 6 **to give os airs** to get high ideas of one's own importance – 9 **rancour** ['ræŋkə] ill feeling, anger – 10 **inevitable** [ɪn'evɪtəbl] unavoidable, having to happen – 11 **destined** determined by fate – 14 **sweeping ascent** rise in one great, uninterrupted movement – 14 **radiant** shining (*here fig*) – 15 **thesis** advanced study done to gain a doctorate (*Doktorarbeit*) – 15 **M.D.** Doctor of Medicine – 16 **select** very special or exclusive – 16 **scholarship** financial aid for study based on high academic merit – 20 **prestigious** highly regarded – 21 **encomium** [en'kəʊmiəm] formal expression of praise – 22 **to relay** to pass on – 25 **to tip** to throw out by lifting one side of the container – 26 **rag-picker** person who collects rags (*Fetzen, Lumpen*) to earn money – 27 **shack** roughly built hut

As for his mother, she gloated chiefly over the strange fact that he had not married in America, had not brought home a foreign wife as all her neighbours had warned her he would, for wasn't that what all Indian boys went abroad for? Instead he agreed, almost without argument, to marry a girl she had picked out for him in her own village, the daughter of a childhood friend, a plump and uneducated girl, it was true, but so old-fashioned, so placid, so complaisant that she slipped into the household and settled in like a charm, seemingly too lazy and too good-natured to even try and make Rakesh leave home and set up independently, as any other girl might have done. What was more, she was pretty – really pretty, in a plump, pudding way that only gave way to fat – soft, spreading fat, like warm wax – after the birth of their first baby, a son, and then what did it matter?

For some years Rakesh worked in the city hospital, quickly rising to the top of the administrative organization, and was made a director before he left to set up his own clinic. He took his parents in his car – a new, sky-blue Ambassador with a rear window full of stickers and charms revolving on strings – to see the clinic when it was built, and the large sign-board over the door on which his name was printed in letters of red, with a row of degrees and qualifications to follow it like so many little black slaves of the regent. Thereafter his fame seemed to grow just a little dimmer – or maybe it was only that everyone in town had grown accustomed to it at last – but it was also the beginning of his fortune for he now became known not only as the best but also the richest doctor in town.

However, all this was not accomplished in the wink of an eye. Naturally not. It was the achievement of a lifetime and it took up Rakesh's whole life. At the time he set up his clinic his father had grown into an old man and retired from his post at the kerosene dealer's depot at which he had worked for forty years, and his mother died soon after, giving up the ghost with a

1 **to gloat** to express smug satisfaction (*sich hämisch freuen*) – 7 **plump** rather fat – 8 **placid** quiet, not expressing any strong feeling – 8 **complaisant** agreeing with the wishes of others – 9 **like a charm** as if by magic – 17 **administrative** concerning management – 19 **Ambassador** Indian make of car – 20 **charm** object meant to bring luck – 23 **degree** academic qualification – 24 **slaves of the regent** ['ri:dʒənt] *here:* an image of a long row (since the regent would have many attendants) – 25 **dim** pale, not so bright – 26 **accustomed to** used to – 29 **to accomplish** to achieve

sigh that sounded positively happy, for it was her own son who ministered to her in her last illness and who sat pressing her feet at the last moment – such a son as few women had borne.

For it had to be admitted – and the most unsuccessful and most rancorous of neighbours eventually did so – that Rakesh was not only a devoted son and a miraculously good-natured man contrived somehow to obey his parents and humour his wife and show concern equally for his children and his patients, but there was actually a brain inside this beautifully polished and formed body of good manners and kind nature and, in between ministering to his family and playing host to many friends and coaxing them all into feeling happy and grateful and content, he had actually trained his hands as well and emerged an excellent doctor, a really fine surgeon. How one man – and a man born to illiterate parents, his father having worked for a kerosene dealer and his mother having spent her life in a kitchen – had achieved, combined and conducted such a medley of virtues, no one could fathom, but all acknowledged his talent and skill.

It was a strange fact, however, that talent and skill, if displayed for too long, cease to dazzle. It came to pass that the most admiring of all eyes eventually faded and no longer blinked at his glory. Having retired from work and having lost his wife, the old father very quickly went to pieces, as they say. He developed so many complaints and fell ill so frequently and with such mysterious diseases that even his son could no longer make out when it was something of significance and when it was merely a peevish whim. He sat huddled on his string bed most of the day and developed an exasperating habit of stretching out suddenly and lying absolutely still, allowing the whole family to fly around him in a flap, wailing and weeping, and then suddenly sitting

2 **to minister to** to take care of – 7 **to contrive** to manage – 7 **to humour sb** to give in to sb's needs and wishes in order to make them happy – 11 **to play host to** to receive as visitors – 12 **to coax** to persuade – 14 **to emerge** to come out; *here:* to finally become – 15 **illiterate** unable to read or write – 18 **medley of virtues** varied mixture of ideals – 18 **to fathom** ['fæðəm] to understand (sth mysterious) – 18 **to acknowledge** to admit, recognize – 21 **to dazzle** to be too bright for one's eyes; *here:* to impress – 21 **to come to pass** to finally happen – 24 **to go to pieces** to fall apart mentally – 28 **peevish** ill-humoured – 28 **whim** frivolous wish – 28 **to huddle** to bend one's body into a small space – 29 **exasperating** very annoying – 31 **in a flap** in great confusion – 31 **to wail** to cry out in sorrow

up, stiff and gaunt, and spitting out a big gob of betel-juice as if to mock their behaviour.

He did this once too often: there had been a big party in the house, a birthday party for the youngest son, and the celebrations had to be suddenly hushed, covered up and hustled out of the way when the daughter-in-law discovered, or thought she discovered, that the old man, stretched out from end to end of his string bed, had lost his pulse; the party broke up, dissolved, even turned into a band of mourners, when the old man sat up and the distraught daughter-in-law received a gob of red spittle right on the hem of her new organza sari. After that no one much cared if he sat up cross-legged on his bed, hawking and spitting, or lay down flat and turned grey as a corpse. Except, of course, for that pearl amongst pearls, his son Rakesh.

It was Rakesh who brought him his morning tea, not in one of the china cups from which the rest of the family drank, but in the old man's favourite brass tumbler, and sat at the edge of his bed, comfortable and relaxed with the string of his pyjamas dangling out from under his fine, lawn night-shirt, and discussed or, rather, read out the morning news to his father. It made no difference to him that his father made no response apart from spitting. It was Rakesh, too, who, on returning from the clinic in the evening, persuaded the old man to come out of his room, as bare and desolate as a cell, and take the evening air out in the garden, beautifully arranging the pillows and bolsters on the divan in the corner of the open verandah. On summer nights he saw to it that the servants carried out the old man's bed onto the lawn and himself helped his father down the steps and onto the bed, soothing him and settling him down for a night under the stars.

All this, was very gratifying for the old man. What was not so gratifying was that he even undertook to supervise his father's diet. One day when the father was really sick, having ordered his

1 **gaunt** very thin and bony – 1 **gob** soft lump – 2 **to mock** to make fun of, ridicule – 9 **band of mourners** people at a funeral – 10 **distraught** very upset – 11 **hem** bottom edge (of clothing) – 13 **to hawk** *here:* to clear one's throst noisily – 14 **corpse** dead body – 18 **brass tumbler** drinking vessel made of a yellow metal – 20 **lawn** *here:* made of a fine cotton or linen – 26 **bolster** ['bəʊlstə] long pillow used to support others – 27 **divan** [dɪ'v□n] backless sofa – 30 **to soothe** [suːð] to make calm – 33 **to supervise** to control, take charge of

daughter-in-law to make him a dish of *soojie halwa* and eaten it with a saucerful of cream, Rakesh marched into the room, not with his usual respectful step but with the confident and rather contemptuous stride of the famous doctor, and declared, 'No more *halwa* for you, papa. We must be sensible, at your age. If you must have something sweet, Veena will cook you a little *kheer*, that's light, just a little rice and milk. But nothing fried, nothing rich. We can't have this happening again.'

The old man who had been lying stretched out on his bed, weak and feeble after a day's illness, gave a start at the very sound, the tone of these words. He opened his eyes – rather, they fell open with shock – and he stared at his son with disbelief that darkened quickly to reproach. A son who actually refused his father the food he craved? No, it was unheard of, it was incredible. But Rakesh had turned his back to him and was cleaning up the litter of bottles and packets on the medicine shelf and did not notice while Veena slipped silently out of the room with a little smirk that only the old man saw, and hated.

Halwa was only the first item to be crossed off the old man's diet. One delicacy after the other went – everything fried to begin with, then everything sweet, and eventually everything, everything that the old man enjoyed. The meals that arrived for him on the shining stainless steel tray twice a day were frugal to say the least – dry bread, boiled lentils, boiled vegetables and, if there were a bit of chicken or fish, that was boiled too. If he called for another helping – in a cracked voice that quavered theatrically – Rakesh himself would come to the door, gaze at him sadly and shake his head, saying, 'Now, papa, we must be careful, we can't risk another illness, you know,' and although the daughter-in-law kept tactfully out of the way, the old man could just see her smirk sliding merrily through the air. He tried to bribe his grand-children into buying him sweets (and how he missed his wife now, that generous, indulgent and illiterate cook), whispering, 'Here's fifty paise,' as he stuffed the coins into a tight, hot fist. 'Run down to the shop at the crossroads

1 **soojie** (*Hindi*) semolina (*Weizengrieß*) – 4 **contemptuous stride** walk expressing superiority and lack of respect – 13 **reproach** blame and complaint – 14 **to crave** to long for, want badly – 18 **smirk** mocking smile – 23 **stainless** *here:* non-rusting – 23 **frugal** very simple – 24 **lentils** vegetable like small, dark peas (*Linsen*) – 26 **to quaver** to shake – 32 **to bribe** to persuade by giving money – 33 **indulgent** very generous – 34 **paise** [peis] (*pl*) Indian coins (each unit worth one hundredth of a rupee)

and buy me thirty paise worth of *jalebis*, and you can spend the remaining twenty paise on yourself. Eh? Understand? Will you do that?' He got away with it once or twice but then was found out, the conspirator was scolded by his father and smacked by his mother and Rakesh came storming into the room, almost tearing his hair as he shouted through compressed lips, 'Now papa, are you trying to turn my little son into a liar? Quite apart from spoiling your own stomach, you are spoiling him as well – you are encouraging him to lie to his own parents. You should have heard the lies he told his mother when she saw him bringing back those *jalebis* wrapped up in filthy newspaper. I don't allow anyone in my house to buy sweets in the bazaar, papa, surely you know that. There's cholera in the city, typhoid, gastroenteritis – I see these cases daily in the hospital, how can I allow my own family to run such risks?' The old man sighed and lay down in the corpse position. But that worried no one any longer.

There was only one pleasure left in the old man now (his son's early morning visits and readings from the newspaper could no longer be called that) and those were visits from elderly neighbours. These were not frequent as his contemporaries were mostly as decrepit and helpless as he and few could walk the length of the road to visit him any more. Old Bhatia, next door, however, who was still spry enough to refuse, adamantly, to bathe in the tiled bathroom indoors and to insist on carrying out his brass mug and towel, in all seasons and usually at impossible hours, into the yard and bathe noisily under the garden tap, would look over the hedge to see if Varma were out on his verandah and would call to him and talk while he wrapped his *dhoti* about him and dried the sparse hair on his head, shivering with enjoyable exaggeration. Of course these conversations, bawled across the hedge by two rather deaf old men conscious of having their entire households overhearing

1 **jalebi** Indian sweet (pretzel-like coils of batter, deep-fried and soaked in syrup) – 4 **conspirator** sb who cooperates in committing a crime – 4 **to scold** to reproach sb, say they have done wrong – 4 **to smack** to hit lightly as punishment – 6 **to compress** to hold tightly together – 8 **to spoil** (*two meanings*) 1. to ruin; 2. to weaken a child's character by being too indulgent – 11 **filthy** very dirty – 14 **gastroenteritis** [ˌgæstrəʊˌentəˈraɪtɪs] an infection of the stomach and intestines – 21 **contemporaries** people of the same generation – 22 **decrepit** [dɪˈkrepɪt] in bad condition – 24 **spry** lively, active – 24 **adamantly** determined, unwilling to change one's mind – 30 **dhoti** (*Hindi*) long loincloth worn by men in India – 30 **sparse** (*of hair*) thin

them, were not very satisfactory but Bhatia occasionally came out of his yard, walked down the bit of road and came in at Varma's gate to collapse onto the stone plinth built under the temple tree. If Rakesh was at home he would help his father down the steps into the garden and arrange him on his night bed under the tree and leave the two old men to chew betel-leaves and discuss the ills of their individual bodies with combined passion.

'At least you have a doctor in the house to look after you,' sighed Bhatia, having vividly described his martyrdom to piles.

'Look after me?' cried Varma, his voice cracking like an ancient clay jar. 'He – he does not even give me enough to eat.'

'What?' said Bhatia, the white hairs in his ears twitching. 'Doesn't give you enough to eat? Your own son?'

'My own son. If I ask him for one more piece of bread, he says no, papa, I weighed out the *ata* myself and I can't allow you to have more than two hundred grams of cereal a day. He weighs the food he gives me, Bhatia – he has scales to weigh it on. That is what it has come to.'

'Never,' murmured Bhatia in disbelief. 'Is it possible, even in this evil age, for a son to refuse his father food?'

'Let me tell you,' Varma whispered eagerly. 'Today the family was having fried fish – I could smell it. I called to my daughter-in-law to bring me a piece. She came to the door and said no....'

'Said no?' It was Bhatia's voice that cracked. A *drongo* shot out of the tree and sped away. *'No?'*

'No, she said no, Rakesh has ordered her to give me nothing fried. No butter, he says, no oil....'

'No butter? No oil? How does he expect his father to live?'

Old Varma nodded with melancholy triumph. 'That is how he treats me – after I have brought him up, given him an education, made him a great doctor. Great doctor! This is the way great doctors treat their fathers, Bhatia,' for the son's

3 **plinth** carved stone (*usu* at the base of a pillar or statue) – 10 **piles** haemorrhoids – 12 **clay** *here:* made of a special kind of earth – 13 **to twitch** to make short, sharp movements – 16 **ata** (*Hindi*) flour – 17 **cereal** food made of wheat or other grain – 22 **eagerly** wanting very much to do sth – 26 **drongo** tropical songbird

sterling personality and character now underwent a curious sea change. Outwardly all might be the same but the interpretation had altered: his masterly efficiency was nothing but cold heartlessness, his authority was only tyranny in disguise.

There was cold comfort in complaining to neighbours and, on such a miserable diet, Varma found himself slipping, weakening and soon becoming a genuinely sick man. Powders and pills and mixtures were not only brought in when dealing with a crisis like an upset stomach but became a regular part of his diet – became his diet, complained Varma, supplanting the natural foods he craved. There were pills to regulate his bowel movements, pills to bring down his blood pressure, pills to deal with his arthritis and, eventually, pills to keep his heart beating. In between there were panicky rushes to the hospital, some humiliating experiences with the stomach pump and enema, which left him frightened and helpless. He cried easily, shrivelling up on his bed, but if he complained of a pain or even a vague, grey fear in the night, Rakesh would simply open another bottle of pills and force him to take one. 'I have my duty to you papa,' he said when his father begged to be let off.

'Let me be,' Varma begged, turning his face away from the pills on the outstretched hand. 'Let me die. It would be better. I do not want to live only to eat your medicines.'

'Papa, be reasonable.'

'I leave that to you,' the father cried with sudden spirit. 'Leave me alone, let me die now, I cannot live like this.'

'Lying all day on his pillows, fed every few hours by his daughter-in-law's own hands, visited by every member of his family daily – and then he says he does not want to live "like this",' Rakesh was heard to say, laughing, to someone outside the door.

'Deprived of food,' screamed the old man on the bed, 'his wishes ignored, taunted by his daughter-in-law, laughed at by his grand-children – *that* is how I live.' But he was very old

1 **sterling** *here:* excellent – 1 **sea change** a seemingly magical transformation (from a song in Shakespeare's *The Tempest*, referring to a body changed by the sea into something different) – 4 **in disguise** [dɪs'gaɪz] dressed up as sth else – 10 **to supplant** to take the place of – 12 **bowel** ['baʊəl] part of to the intestines (organs which absorb food and excrete remains) – 15 **humiliating** *here:* embarrassing – 16 **enema** ['enɪmə] medicine inserted into the rectum – 17 **to shrivel** ['ʃrɪvl] to shrink (*usu* of a plant: to dry up and become smaller) – 32 **to deprive** to make sb do without sth – 33 **to taunt** to mock

and weak and all anyone heard was an incoherent croak, some expressive grunts and cries of genuine pain. Only once, when old Bhatia had come to see him and they sat together under the temple tree, they heard him cry, 'God is calling me – and they won't let me go.'

The quantities of vitamins and tonics he was made to take were not altogether useless. They kept him alive and even gave him a kind of strength that made him hang on long after he ceased to wish to hang on. It was as though he were straining at a rope, trying to break it, and it would not break, it was still strong. He only hurt himself, trying.

In the evening, that summer, the servants would come into his cell, grip his bed, one at each end, and carry it out to the verandah, there setting it down with a thump that jarred every tooth in his head. In answer to his agonized complaints they said the doctor sahib had told them he must take the evening air and the evening air they would make him take – thump. Then Veena, that smiling, hypocritical pudding in a rustling sari, would appear and pile up the pillows under his head till he was propped up stiffly into a sitting position that made his head swim and his back ache.

'Let me lie down,' he begged. 'I can't sit up any more.'

'Try, papa, Rakesh said you can if you try,' she said, and drifted away to the other end of the verandah where her transistor radio vibrated to the lovesick tunes from the cinema that she listened to all day.

So there he sat, like some stiff corpse, terrified, gazing out on the lawn where his grand-sons played cricket, in danger of getting one of their hard-spun balls in his eye, and at the gate that opened onto the dusty and rubbish-heaped lane but still bore, proudly, a newly touched-up signboard that bore his son's name and qualifications, his own name having vanished from the gate long ago.

At last the sky-blue Ambassador arrived, the cricket game broke up in haste, the car drove in smartly and the doctor, the great doctor, all in white, stepped out. Someone ran up to take

1 **incoherent** [ˌɪnkəʊˈhɪərənt] not making sense, hard to interpret – 1 **croak** rough vocal sound – 14 **to jar** to have a painful effect on – 15 **agonized** full of pain – 16 **sahib** (*Hindi*) term of respect for a man – 18 **hypocritical** [ˌhɪpəˈkrɪtɪkəl] not sincere – 18 **to rustle** to make a soft, light sound – 20 **to prop up** to give support to, in order to keep erect – 31 **touched-up** improved by adding fresh paint – 32 **to vanish** to disappear

his bag from him, others to escort him up the steps. 'Will you have tea?' his wife called, turning down the transistor set, 'Or a Coca-Cola? Shall I fry you some *samosas*?' But he did not reply or even glance in her direction. Ever a devoted son, he went first to the corner where his father sat gazing, stricken, at some undefined spot in the dusty yellow air that swam before him. He did not turn his head to look at his son. But he stopped gobbling air with his uncontrolled lips and set his jaw as hard as a sick and very old man could set it.

'Papa,' his son said, tenderly, sitting down on the edge of the bed and reaching out to press his feet.

Old Varma tucked his feet under him, out of the way, and continued to gaze stubbornly into the yellow air of the summer evening.

'Papa, I'm home.'

Varma's hand jerked suddenly, in a sharp, derisive movement, but he did not speak.

'How are you feeling, papa?'

Then Varma turned and looked at his son. His face was so out of control and all in pieces, that the multitude of expressions that crossed it could not make up a whole and convey to the famous man exactly what his father thought of him, his skill, his art.

'I'm dying,' he croaked. 'Let me die, I tell you.'

'Papa, you're joking,' his son smiled at him, lovingly. 'I've brought you a new tonic to make you feel better. You must take it, it will make you feel stronger again. Here it is. Promise me you will take it regularly, papa.'

Varma's mouth worked as hard as though he still had a gob of betel in it (his supply of betel had been cut off years ago). Then he spat out some words, as sharp and bitter as poison, into his son's face. 'Keep your tonic – I want none – I want none – I won't take any more of – of your medicines. None. Never,' and he swept the bottle out of his son's hand with a wave of his own, suddenly grand, suddenly effective.

3 **samosa** Indian snack (meat and/or vegetables wrapped in pastry) – 5 **stricken** struck by some shocking thought – 7 **to gobble** to (try to) swallow fast – 10 **tender** kind and loving – 13 **stubborn** ['stʌbən] very determined, hard to persuade – 16 **to jerk** to make a sudden sharp movement – 16 **derisive** [dɪ'raɪsɪv] expressing contempt – 20 **multitude** great number – 21 **to convey** to get one's meaning across, make sb understand – 26 **tonic** medicinal drink

His son jumped, for the bottle was smashed and thick brown syrup had splashed up, staining his white trousers. His wife let out a cry and came running. All around the old man was hubbub once again, noise, attention.

He gave one push to the pillows at his back and dislodged them so he could sink down on his back, quite flat again. He closed his eyes and pointed his chin at the ceiling, like some dire prophet, groaning, 'God is calling me – now let me go.'

3 **hubbub** confusion – 5 **to dislodge** to remove from a fixed position – 8 **dire** terrible

Meher Pestonji

About the Author

Born in 1946 into the Parsi community of Bombay, **Meher Pestonji** does not strongly identify with this community, but has caused considerable controversy by her criticism of what she regards as their elitist attitudes.

Despite the disapproval of her upper-middle class family, she worked for years among the street children and slum dwellers of her city, campaigning for better housing rights, and (in the 1970s) a change in rape law.

After her marriage broke up, she became a freelance journalist to support her two daughters. She provided detailed reporting on the SriKrishan Commission instituted to investigate the Bombay riots of 1992-93. Her own encounter with the bloodshed and grief caused by these riots was the most intense experience of her life.

The story included here is from her first collection of fiction, *Mixed Marriage and Other Parsi Stories* (1999). Since then, she has had two novels published: *Pervez* (2002), which explores the topics of inter-communal prejudice and social privilege; and *Sadak Chaap* (2006), which has been praised for the unrelenting realism and deep sympathy with which she evokes the brutal existance of street children.

Meher Pestonji continues to campaign for social justice, and has most recently been involved in awareness programmes for the rights of HIV-infected people and their spouses.

Meher Pestonji

Outsider

Theresa slammed the door behind her, flung her bag onto the bed and stormed into the bathroom to splash water on her red, hot face. As the tap gushed onto her sweater she peeled it off, threw it into a basin of soap-suds and smacked handfuls of cold water on her cheeks, neck, breasts. A few minutes of this helped her cool down. She shut off the tap, continuing to stand in the bathroom, the waist band of her jeans absorbing drops from rivulets running down her body.

Sinking her face into the softness of a towel she looked for a T-shirt. There wasn't one in the bathroom but it didn't matter. Her bedroom door was shut. Though the curtains were not drawn, the expanse of sea afforded more privacy than the locked door.

Topless, she walked to the window, inhaling deeply. Breathe in, hold, breathe out, hold, breathe in, as she'd learnt in yoga. Thirty-odd breaths later she felt the calm returning. Only then did she realise that her eyes were still shut.

She opened them to catch a flock of seagulls take off from the waters around Mahalaxmi temple, a tiny offshore island connected to the city by a narrow footpath thronged by Hindu and Muslim devotees at all times of the day. The sight never failed to delight her. With the sun about to dip into the western horizon, pink flecks circled the sea in sweeping curves before coming to rest on the dome, minarets and on the bobbing waves. She often wondered how gulls flew so close without wings crashing into tragedies. But in the four months she had been observing them from her window at Eden Hall not once had there been an accident.

She looked into the mirror to find her face no longer flushed. Sitting on the bed she pulled off her jeans and went back into the bathroom for a shower. As needles of cold water beat against her head and back she felt the last dregs of tension ease.

1 **to slam** to close with a bang – 1 **to fling, flung** to throw violently – 3 **to gush** [gʌʃ] to pour out suddenly – 3 **to peel** to remove carefully like the skin of a fruit – 4 **suds** foam formed by soap in water – 4 **to smack** to apply with a hitting movement – 8 **rivulet** streams of water – 11 **drawn** *here:* closed – 12 **expanse** wide stretch – 12 **to afford** *here:* to give, provide – 13 **topless** undressed from the waist up – 19 **thronged** [θrɒŋd] crowded – 20 **devotee** [ˌdevəʊˈtiː] religious follower – 23 **dome** large hemispherical roof (*usu* of a church) – 23 **to bob** to move lightly up and down – 28 **flushed** (*of a face*) red and hot – 31 **dregs** sth left over (*usu* scraps of food, liquid, etc.)

She shouldn't have lost her temper so impetuously, she told herself. Cawas and Zenia had been decent with her. They were a young couple from the privileged strata of society and since she was in India to study the underprivileged, contrasts were bound to surface. In two months she'd be back in Munich and have time to reflect on her divergent experiences of India.

Reaching for a towel she rubbed herself dry slipping into the cotton kaftan she'd bought on her first day in Bombay. The green and white print offset her red-brown hair highlighting her blue-green eyes. She rubbed moisturiser on her face, hands, legs, then went back to the window watching lights come on in skyscrapers across the bay. Eden Hall had one of the best views in Bombay. The sea, licking the edges of a curved boulevard dotted with speeding cars beyond which she could see the emerald green turf where horse races were held on weekends.

There was a knock at the door and Zenia called 'Ready for a drink?'

'Coming,' she replied, conscious that such social niceties were not part of the paying guest contract which covered only the room, breakfast and dinner. Their generosity made them include her in their social life, getting her invited to the homes of their friends and taken on weekends to the countryside. Her Bombay visit would have been far more austere had she not been staying with the Shroffs.

She found Cawas in the drawing room furnished with blue-green upholstery and matching drapes, blue and white chinaware displayed in a showcase along the wall. 'Beer for you as usual?' he asked and was about to pop a can of Kingfisher when she stopped him.

'I'll have gin and tonic today,' she said. 'I need something cool.'

'Beer's cool.'

1 **impetuous** [ɪm'petjʊəs] impulsive, without thinking – 2 **decent** ['di:sənt] *here:* friendly, well-meaning – 3 **strata** (*pl*) levels (*here:* of social class) – 5 **to surface** to emerge, come to the surface – 6 **divergent** [daɪ'vɜ:dʒənt] very different – 9 **to offset** to contrast with pleasantly – 10 **moisturiser** cream to keep the skin soft – 15 **emerald** (the colour of) a green precious stone – 15 **turf** area of very short grass (*usu* for sport) – 18 **nicety** ['naɪsɪtɪ] fine point of behaviour – 20 **generosity** generous behaviour, i.e. giving freely – 23 **austere** very simple and frugal – 25 **drawing room** formal sitting room – 26 **upholstery** soft parts of furniture – 26 **drapes** curtains – 27 **chinaware** fine porcelain – 28 **to pop** *here:* to open – 28 **Kingfisher** brand of Indian beer

'That's what Indians say. In Germany we have beer in winter. Anyway Cawas, I want to apologise. I shouldn't have lost my shirt as I did.'

'Apology unnecessary,' he replied, brushing aside her discomfort. 'Foreigners are over-sensitive to poverty. We are innoculated against it from birth. Vaccinations against polio, tuberculosis and the invisible vaccine that blinds us to unsightly images. Without the last vaccine we'd be miserable every day of our lives. Don't you think we need it in India?'

She squirmed at his condescension but there was also some truth in what he said. The Indian rich seemed unperturbed by the inhuman conditions in which people lived barely yards away from themselves. The blind spot may be a survival strategy as Cawas implied but Theresa felt it just wasn't right.

She thought it prudent not to enter into an argument but the next day narrated the incident to Jyoti who was the guide for her doctorate thesis. A sociology student Theresa was documenting the lives of streetchildren in Bombay while her research associates did the same with streetchildren in Rio de Janeiro, Johannesburg and Kuala Lumpur after which they planned a comprehensive analysis.

Jyoti had taken her step by step, introducing her to railway stations where runaway kids arrive in Bombay, to the beaches and bazaars where they sometimes find employment, to the free food distribution centres attached to places of worship, to the rubbish bins that hold treasures like throwaway combs for ragpickers, to streetcorners called addas where kids as young as ten got high on pot, drinks, drugs and even by smelling the glue used by cobblers to seal the soles of shoes, and finally to the shelters run by nongovernment organisations where kids are free to come and go while social workers monitor their activities stepping in to intervene when necessary.

2 **to lose one's shirt** *here fig:* to lose control and get angry – 5 **discomfort** *here:* embarrassment – 6 **to inoculate** to vaccinate, i.e. make resistant to a disease by introducing into the body a weakened form of the agent that causes it – 7 **unsightly** unpleasant to look at – 10 **to squirm** to move or shrink with embarrassment – 10 **condescension** patronizing behaviour towards sb on a lower level – 11 **unperturbed** not bothered – 15 **prudent** wise – 16 **to narrate** to tell (a story) – 19 **associate** sb working on the same task – 21 **comprehensive** overall, covering all aspects – 25 **worship** religious service – 27 **ragpicker** sb who collects old rags, i.e. torn pieces of clothing – 28 **pot** (*inf*) cannabis, marijuana – 29 **cobbler** shoemaker – 29 **to seal** to attach securely and make water-resistant

Theresa had been told to anticipate dirt and poverty in India but was unprepared for the resilience and buoyancy of these kids who seemed more prepared for life than streetkids in the west. They were street smart with a cockiness that comes from being your own boss from an early age. Some were as young as eight or nine, looking even younger due to malnutrition. Yet they'd learnt to survive in a big-fish-eat-little-fish environment where they were the smallest fish of all.

'The boy came up to the car at the traffic lights, wiped the windshield with a duster then tapped Cawas' window asking for a tip,' Theresa told Jyoti the day after she'd stormed off from the car. 'Cawas told him to get lost. When I took out some money from my handbag he stopped me. "Don't encourage beggars. They work in gangs to fleece honest citizens like us," he said. Just then the lights changed and he stepped on the accelerator though the boy's hand was still on the car. "That boy might have been killed! In Germany you'd be arrested for doing that!" I cried, turning back to see the boy jumping onto a road-divider. Do you know what he said, Jyoti? I remember his exact words ... he said, "The son-of-a-bitch knows how to take care of himself. Anyway there are millions of chhokra-boys around. One more or less makes no difference." I was so shocked! I called him a bastard without a conscience and jumped out of the car. I don't know how I'm going to survive these people for two more months.'

'You don't have to live there. If you want we can find you hostel accommodation,' said Jyoti who, after four months, was familiar with Theresa's outbursts.

Theresa fell silent. Eden Hall was the most luxurious apartment she had ever lived in. Nowhere in Europe could she have afforded such a place. Only the dollar exchange rate made it possible. And despite the clash of ideals she wanted to taste the pleasures of India even while studying her slums.

1 **to anticipate** [□n'tɪsɪpeɪt] to expect – 2 **resilience** [rɪ'zɪlɪəns] ability to resist pressure and bounce back (*here fig*) – 2 **buoyancy** ability to float (*here fig*) – 4 **cockiness** confident attitude, showing little respect for authority – 6 **malnutrition** ill health caused by lack of food – 10 **to tap** to touch lightly with the hand – 14 **to fleece** to remove all the wool of a sheep; *here fig:* to rob – 15 **accelerater** [□k'seləreɪtə] gas pedal – 20 **son-of-a-bitch** (*inf, vulg*) bad man or boy (*Hurensohn*) – 21 **chhokra** (*Hindi; usu derog*) boy, youngster – 23 **bastard** (*inf, vulg*) bad man or boy – 23 **conscience** part of one's mind that tells right from wrong – 32 **clash** conflict

She had got sucked into the Shroffs' social whirl within a week of moving into Eden Hall. Cawas was short and stocky with a pointed French beard while his wife was petite, with cow-like eyes and frizzy hair fanning her heart-shaped face. They were part of a group of wealthy Parsis who met each week for dinner at one another's places. The men were practising lawyers, doctors or in managerial positions with leading private companies while the women worked in ad agencies, airlines or as secretaries to business magnates. Every two or three weeks they would take off for a weekend at the seaside or a hill station and periodically they would book a couple of rows in a cinema house where they'd troop in to see a popular film like Titanic.

Initially Theresa was flattered to find herself the centre of attention. Not only did the men keep her glass filled and escort her to the dining table introducing her to exotic Parsi cuisine where fish came wrapped in banana leaves and chicken was cooked with dry apricots topped with potato straws, they also included her in their friendly banter where the game of one-upmanship was acted out in verbal sparring. After a few weeks, however, she began finding the banter banal, with jokes being repeated long after the punch lines had lost their bite, as in family Christmas gatherings. Only these gatherings happened every week.

'Nice aunty,' someone might say while driving past an attractive young girl.

'Yours or mine?' would come the response.

'You make her your aunty, I'll pull down her panty!' and the group would dissolve into peals of laughter. The first time it sounded funny but as wit sank into stereotype Theresa thought people chorusing the last line sounded like a children's recitation class.

1 **whirl** constant circling movement (*here fig*) – 2 **stocky** short and solidly built – 4 **frizzy** very curly – 4 **to fan** *here:* to spread around like a fan (*Fächer*) – 5 **Parsi** member the Zoroastrian community in India, descendant of those who emigrated from Persia after the 7th century Islamic conquest – 10 **hill station** summer resort in the hills – 12 **to troop** to move in a large group (like an army) – 13 **initially** at first – 13 **flattered** pleased to be highly regarded or admired – 14 **to escort** to formally accompany – 15 **cuisine** (*French*) style of cooking – 18 **banter** amusing small-talk – 18 **one-upmanship** trying to make fun of each other and gain the advantage – 19 **to spar** to act as if fighting (like boxers practising) – 21 **punch line** end of a joke that makes the point clear – 28 **to dissolve** to melt, break down (*here fig*) – 28 **peal** sound like that of a bell – 29 **wit** cleverness at making jokes – 30 **to chorus** to speak together as if joining in the chorus of a song

Unlike Jyoti who wore a saree or the loose-fitting shalwaar-kameez, the women in this group all wore western clothes. They had holidayed in the west and were more keen on reliving their travel experiences with a foreigner than on informing her about local history or customs of which they seemed ill informed. During the Ganpati festival, when the entire city reverberated to drums, music and chants of 'Ganpati bappa moriya' as giant sized clay idols of the elephant god were immersed into the sea, they complained about the noise and traffic jams but could not tell her about the myth surrounding Ganesh. Their lives seemed centred around acquiring imported cosmetics, French perfumes and Swiss chocolates and cheese.

One pretty girl was an air hostess providing a steady supply of goodies to them all. One evening she announced she had bought five bottles of Yves St Laurent's Opium to find nine women clamouring for them.

'If Opium smells like opium it must be deadly,' quipped a man in a red checked shirt.

'If Opium tastes like opium it would be deadlier,' responded another in a safari suit.

'If Opium is opium it's a killer and will take our lovely ladies to never-never-land!' climaxed a third, as Theresa, who'd just seen an emaciated boy struggle through withdrawal, debated whether or not such jokes were in bad taste.

She had started working as a volunteer at a day and night shelter to get an insight into the world of streetkids, handing out medicines for cuts, coughs, diarrhoea, engaging them in painting and clay modelling, listening to their case histories with the help of a translator. Most kids used the shelter only to sleep at night, going about their business of washing cars, hawking, sweeping, ragpicking during the day. Some came twice or three

1 **saree** = sari, Indian dress made of one long piece of cloth – 1 **shalwar-kameez** women's suit consisting of trousers and long tunic – 6 **Ganpati** Hindu feast in honour of Ganesh, the elephant-like god – 6 **to reverberate** to echo, reflect the sound – 7 **chant** words spoken rhythmically, *usu* with a religious significance – 7 **Ganpati bappa moriya** (*Marathi*) Ganpati, My Lord/Father (meaning of last word is unclear) – 8 **clay** made of a kind of earth – 8 **to immerse** to put into water (or other liquid) – 14 **goodies** (*inf*) nice things – 15 **Yves ... Opium** perfume marketed by a French fashion designer – 16 **to clamour** to call out for noisily – 17 **to quip** to joke – 22 **to climax** to reach or achieve the highest point – 23 **emaciated** extremely thin from hunger – 23 **withdrawal** *here:* giving up an addictive drug – 27 **diarrhoea** [ˌdaɪəˈriːə] disorder of the intestines causing uncontrolled bowel movements (*Durchfall*) – 30 **to hawk** to sell on the street

times a week, others barely twice a month. Santosh was the only boy she could communicate with, for he spoke a smattering of English.

He had recently arrived from Almora, at the foothills of the Himalayas. His father was a government school teacher, drinking himself to oblivion each evening, often beating and sexually assaulting his wife as Santosh and his sister cowered in a corner. When the twelve year old could take it no more he flung a large stone at his father, then, seeing the older man slump in a stupor, had fled.

'How did you learn English?' she asked Santosh in her heavily accented English which the boy had some difficulty following.

'In Almora Christian School. I study seven class Hindi. From four class we do English. One hour Father Bosco make class talk English only. On train English useful for TC.'

'What's TC?'

'Ticket-walla. I no buy ticket. When TC come I say I servant boy. Memsahib have ticket in first class. If you say in English TC believes. Or make me get off train. Wait in jungle for other train.'

'Don't you want to go home, Santosh?'

'No, didi. I scared. If baba dead I go jail. I make money in Mumbai. Call ma here. Sister also.'

'If your father is dead your mother might need you.'

'Not like that. If I go she send me school and work-work to feed me. Now she feed only sister.'

Before she could probe deeper Jyoti intervened. 'Santosh will go into depression if he thinks too much about his family. Now cheer him up.'

Theresa took him to a fruit juice stall but Santosh opted for an ice cream. Seeing him lick the fast melting dribbles off his fingers she offered him a second. 'No, didi, you no have. How I can have two? Thenkyu.'

2 **smattering** small amount of – 6 **oblivion** state of unconsciousness – 7 **to assault** to attack – 7 **to cower** to crouch in fear – 10 **to slump** to sink or fall heavily – 10 **stupor** state of being drunk and unconscious – 10 **to flee, fled** to run away – 13 **Hindi** official language of India (probably not Santosh's first language) – 17 **walla** (*Hindi*) person responsible for a certain job; *here:* collector – 18 **memsahib** (*Hindi*) term of respect for a high-ranking lady – 22 **didi** form of address for Hindi 'elder sister' – 22 **baba** child's term for 'father' in many Indian languages – 23 **Mumbai** now offical name of Bombay – 27 **to probe** to examine, try to get information – 30 **stall** market stand – 30 **to opt** to choose – 31 **dribble** liquid flowing accidentally from food

Contrasted against this Cawas' attitude seemed unforgivable.

An earlier instance of their group's insensitivity was clearly etched in Theresa's memory. Four carloads had gone for a weekend to a lakeside. Adults, kids and pedigreed dogs piled into cars that whizzed along the highway overtaking petrol tankers and trucks at breathtaking speed. Theresa was used to speed but not the haphazard traffic where bicyclists and pedestrians clung to the edge of the same road as speeding vehicles which had to be as prepared for an ambling cow as for the dog who might jump out of the bushes in a frenzy of aggressive barking.

The lake waters were soothing after the drive. As the others unloaded cars in front of the bungalow where they would spend the night Theresa waded into the water and was delighted to find her toes tickled by tiny fish. She bent down, cupping her hands to trap the barely visible shimmering streaks, laughing each time they slipped away.

'Use my handkerchief,' called Savak tossing her a large kerchief with a grey border. Theresa dipped it in the water, raising it to find two silver slivers gasping for breath. Immediately she lowered it again. 'Didn't you get anything?' he asked.

'They're tiny. Too small to eat.'

'Catch them for fun.'

'It stops being funny when they die.'

'You're soft-hearted. I thought German girls were tough.'

'Tough doesn't mean you have to be cruel.'

Savak paired up with her for that weekend, carrying her rucksack, helping her across moss-covered rocks, guiding the way to the waterfall where they gazed at the slow cascading froth that appeared deceptively gentle. He was a burly sixfooter with shaggy eyebrows shading sharp eyes and a long aquiline nose. Together they carried one of the large hampers of food to the base of the waterfall. Sandwiches, sausages, lamb-chops and omelettes were passed around as children gorged on Coke

4 **to etch** to cut a pattern into metal (*here fig*) – 5 **pedigreed** with a documented pure-bred ancestry – 8 **haphazard** [ˌh□p'h□zəd] unorganized, chaotic – 10 **to amble** to walk slowly in a relaxed way – 11 **frenzy** wild excitement – 12 **to soothe** [su:ð] to make calm – 14 **to wade** to walk into water – 16 **to shimmer** to shine unsteadily – 20 **sliver** little thin piece – 29 **to cascade** (*of water, etc.*) to fall with great force – 30 **froth** [frɒθ] lots of fine bubbles (on top of water, etc.) – 30 **burly** big, heavily built – 31 **shaggy** bushy, untidy – 31 **aquiline** curved like an eagle's beak – 34 **to gorge on** to eat or drink huge amounts

and potato chips. Theresa sat perched on a rock under an overhanging tree, listening to the sound of gurgling water mingle with the laughter of children aiming stones at a chameleon on a large rock. When a tin of Mackintosh toffees was opened five year old Nishat threw her wrapper into the water only to be pulled up and made to fish it out. All the litter, including empty Coke bottles, paper cups and plates was collected and carried back to the cars.

They were ready to return to the city when someone remembered the cheese sandwiches. Nobody, not even the dogs with their happy wagging tails, wanted any more. Theresa had noticed a bunch of skinny kids when they arrived but Cawas had shooed them away threatening to set the dogs after them. 'These blighters steal ACs and stereos from cars,' he told Theresa, seeing the expression on her face.

Theresa's heart had ached for the bedraggled kids and now she volunteered to take them the leftover food.

'No, no, not those dirty children,' said a busty woman whose thighs bulged below clinging shorts.

'Aren't there any dogs?' asked another.

'The dogs have all eaten.'

'Not our dogs. Mountain dogs. We always give stray dogs the leftovers.'

'Why not give leftovers to kids!'

'They're full of lice! They never have a bath!'

'How do you know?'

'We live here so we know. Foreigners are too sentimental.'

Theresa was angry at being put down and felt revolted as she saw the fat woman feeding a scrawny dog while a boy and a girl with bamboo stick legs and sun bleached hair watched enviously. The next day she shared her disgust with Jyoti who took it stoically. 'I know the class divide is bad but I didn't realise

1 **to perch** to sit like a bird on sth – 2 **to mingle** to mix – 4 **Mackintosh** brand of English toffees – 5 **wrapper** paper or plastic covering – 12 **skinny** very thin – 13 **to shoo** (*inf*) to to try to send away with a gesture – 14 **blighter** (*inf, derog*) fellow – 14 **AC** = air conditioning equipment – 16 **bedraggled** dirty and badly dressed – 18 **busty** with large breasts – 19 **to bulge** to swell outwards – 19 **to cling** to stick tightly – 25 **lice** *pl* of 'louse' – 28 **to put sb down** to say sth mocking or derogatory to sb – 28 **revolted** feeling disgust (*Abscheu*) – 29 **scrawny** (*derog*) extremely thin – 32 **stoically** without showing much feeling (from the ancient Greek Stoic philosophy)

that some people prioritise stray dogs over starving human beings,' she said drily.

When Santosh discovered she lived at Eden Hall which was only a thirty minute walk from the shelter he would often come for a dip in the ocean and they would walk back together. Reaching the seafront an hour earlier, he'd clamber over rocks to the water's edge, strip down to a G-string and wash his clothes, scrubbing and beating them against rocks to loosen particles of dirt. Spreading them out to dry he'd splash among the waves before hauling himself out to dry in the sun like his clothes.

Sometimes he would bring Theresa a gift from the sea. Shells, coconut kernels curled into unusual shapes and once a live crab. Theresa refused to touch the crab so Santosh, with mischief sparkling in his eyes, ran all the way to the shelter dangling the wriggling creature between his fingers. For the rest of the day he chased kids around with the crab till it ended its life in a pot of boiling aromatic spices.

He never walked straight, bounding ahead with restless energy, a grin on his impish face. His eyes were constantly darting, searching for bottle caps to be scooped out of gutters or pavement corners near cold drink stalls. Theresa first thought he was collecting Pepsi, Gold Spot, Mangola caps the way kids collect stamps, to discover that for Santosh these were a source of livelihood. Each week he would take them to a recycling centre, haggle over the price, then treat himself to the latest Hindi film. When the haul was good he'd also splurge on mutton biryani, cooked in huge pots on the street by women at Grant Road near the cinema houses he frequented.

Savak started calling her up after the picnic. He invited her for a violin recital for which he had received complimentary tickets from his bank, to go jogging at Mahalaxmi race course

1 **to prioritise** to give priority to, i.e. put first – 6 **to clamber** to climb awkwardly – 7 **G-string** very minimal underpants – 10 **to haul** to pull – 13 **mischief** ['mɪstʃɪf] playful behaviour that causes (or seems to cause) trouble – 14 **to dangle** to let hang – 15 **to wriggle** to make twisting movements – 17 **spice** tasty additions to food (e.g. pepper, chilli) – 18 **to bound** to move in large jumps – 19 **impish** like an imp (*Kobold*), i.e. expressing mischief – 20 **to dart** to make short, sharp movements – 20 **to scoop** to lift out with a round movement of the hands or some other instrument – 20 **gutter** low part at the side of a road (for draining water away) – 24 **livelihood** money to live on – 25 **to haggle** to argue about the price – 26 **to splurge** to enjoy sth expensive as a special treat – 26 **mutton biriyani** rice dish including pieces of mutton (the meat of a sheep) – 30 **complimentary** *here:* free

which she could see from her eleventh floor window, to sample lobsters at Trishna, a popular sea-food restaurant. Like all Zenia and Cawas' friends he was proud of being a Parsi and lost no opportunity to impress his community's heritage on her.

'We are not dark, like Indians, because we come from Persia. We had to flee from there because of Islamic persecution,' he told her. 'When our ancestors landed at Sanjan thirteen hundred years ago the Hindu king granted asylum on certain conditions – that we adopt the local language and dress, that we don't intermarry with the local population and don't convert them to our religion. So to this day non-Parsis are not allowed to enter fire-temples,' he'd say pointing to fire-temples with the winged-bull symbol as they drove past.

'We are an endangered species, with barely a hundred thousand Parsis left in the world,' he told her another time. 'While Indians breed more and more, Parsis breed less and less. Parsi panchayat is actually giving incentives to young couples to have more children but it's having little effect. Who wants panchayat trustees interfering in family affairs!'

After dinner at Trishna he took her walking around the Fort area pointing out monumental floodlit buildings with Gothic columns and arches. 'All these are built by the Cawasji Jehangir family,' he told her. 'Elphinstone College, the University Convocation Hall, Jehangir Art Gallery, and the C. J. Hall which has recently been converted to the Gallery of Modern Art. We Parsis built Bombay with the help of the British. See how these ghaatis have ruined it after the Britishers left!' Ghaati she was to learn, was a derisive term for the local Maharashtrian population.

On another evening he spoke of Jamshetji Jejeebhoy who more than a century ago founded premier institutions for art and architecture and also built a hospital for lower and middle

1 **to sample** to try out – 4 **heritage** sth received from one's ancestors – 6 **persecution** systematic bad or cruel treatment (of a group) – 7 **Sanjan** region of the north-west Indian State of Gujarat – 12 **fire temple** Parsi place of worship (being Zoroastrians, they revere fire as a symbol of Ahura Mazda, the god of creation) – 14 **endangered species** category of plant or animal in danger of dying out (*here fig*) – 16 **to breed** to have children – 17 **panchayat** (*Hindi*) council of elders – 22 **arch** rounded doorway or passage – 22 **Cawasji** = 'Cawas' plus the respectful suffix '-ji'; similarly, 'Jamshetji', l. 30 – 24 **convocation** important gathering; *here (Indian use):* degree-giving ceremony – 28 **derisive** derogatory, mocking – 28 **Maharashtrian** of Maharashtra, the State including Bombay/Mumbai – 31 **premier** first-class

class patients of all communities. ‘Lady Jejeebhoy constructed the Mahim Causeway connecting two of Bombay’s seven islands from private funds and refused to charge a toll since that would make the arterial road inaccessible to the poor,’ said Savak, his voice swelling with pride. ‘Jamshetji Jejeebhoy was knighted by the British for his philanthropy. After him people coined the phrase “Parsi thy name is charity”.’

‘You’re always talking about the past. What great works are Parsis doing today?’ she asked.

‘The Tatas are the most respected business house of the country,’ he replied. They started the first steel plant in India, the first hydro-electric works, the first engineering works. All before Independence. Planning for the future of the country. And now Ratan Tata has designed India’s first indigenous car. From their profits they built the best cancer hospital in the country, founded an institute for social sciences, another for research in the fundamental sciences. Imagine doing all this without black money in a country like India!’

‘But what about average Parsis? Are they all as effete and as pleasure-loving as your friends?’

‘Parsis love the good life. And our religion encourages it. We are not expected to be ascetic like Hindus.’

‘How can a community be considered charitable and yet be so blind to the poorest of the poor?’

‘The community takes pride in looking after its own. I can say with confidence that you won’t find a single Parsi living in those huts or slums. I don’t know why you keep going there. Why didn’t you come to India to study something useful like architecture or the flora-fauna of the Himalayas.’

‘My work is useful. It is also satisfying.’

‘It’s all right if you’re earning dollars. Do you know what Indian social workers get?’

2 **causeway** road or passage built through water – 3 **funds** money – 4 **arterial** major, connecting many minor roads (*from* ‘artery’, a major blood vessel) – 4 **inaccessible** impossible to reach or use – 5 **to knight** to make a knight, with the title ‘Sir’ – 6 **philanthropy** [fɪ'l□nθrəpɪ] generous practice of charity – 10 **Tatas** Tata family – 13 **Independence** end of British rule, 1947 – 14 **indigenous** [ɪn'dɪdʒɪnəs] native to a particular place – 19 **effete** [ɪ'fi:t] weak and decadent – 22 **ascetic** [ə'setɪk] living simply without comfort and pleasure

It hadn't occurred to her to compare salaries with Jyoti. 'Money isn't everything. You must believe in and enjoy what you're doing.'

'You enjoy going to those dirty areas?'

'Yes I do. Not the dirt but the fighting spirit of the kids inspires me. Their survival instinct is so strong. They travel to Bombay from all over the country with only a dream in their hearts. A dream to make big in a big city. A dream to hit the floodlights. A dream to be in the same city as their favourite filmstar … And perhaps peep into her car at a traffic junction … They've left behind homes and families in search of that dream. That's courage.'

'It's insane. The city gets burdened with their dirty, sloppy ways and sentimental foreigners sing paeans to the filthy monsters.'

She gave up. He was incapable of looking beyond the dirt and grime of physical reality. Yet she continued accepting his invitations despite knowing their divergent views on almost every subject.

'You walk too slow-slow, didi,' Santosh would say as she struggled with her dupatta in the breeze. When she was with Savak or the Shroffs she wore her German skirts and jeans but at the shelter she felt cooler in the loose shalwaar-kameez enjoying the soft feel of the dupatta around her shoulders. But this scarf-like garment was not easy to control when it was windy and unless she anchored it around her neck till it almost throttled her it threatened to fly away.

'Not good to fall dupatta, didi. You my sister. Not that kind girl.' She couldn't figure out what he was getting at. Each time he'd insist she straighten out her clothing before entering the shelter. And get visibly upset if she didn't. Finally she asked Jyoti.

'Dropping the dupatta or pulav of a saree is a way of attracting men,' she laughed. It's a common gesture in old Hindi films.'

'But I'm fully covered underneath!'

1 **to occur to sb** to think of – 10 **to peep** to take a quick look into sth – 13 **insane** mad, crazy – 13 **sloppy** carelessly messy – 14 **paean** ['piːən] hymn of praise (*here fig*) – 17 **grime** dirt on the surface of sth – 18 **divergent** very different, opposing – 21 **dupatta** part of the tunic of a shalwaar-kameez, worn over head or neck (as is the 'pulav' of a sari, l. 33) – 26 **to anchor** ['□ŋkə] to fix securely (as does the anchor of a boat) – 26 **to throttle** to choke, prevent from breathing by pressing on the neck

'Santosh is from the conservative north. He feels protective about you. To him dropping your dupatta is like cheapening yourself.'

'He's only a kid! How can he be so patriarchal!'

She was perplexed. How could fully covered breasts be considered more provocative than the bare midriff between the sarees and cholis most women wore, she wondered.

Acknowledging a special bond with Santosh she often carried down the fruit from her breakfast tray for him. At high tide she would have breakfast to the boom-swish of the waves. She would watch the graceful gliding gulls diving between rocks to fish in the shallows.

She had told Santosh she would be returning to Germany soon, but as the time neared she found herself concerned about his future. Other kids resented the special attention he received from her. Some abused him even in her presence. More than once Jyoti warned her, 'The boys are hungry for love. If you become a mother-figure for Santosh it'll be terrible for him when you leave.' Theresa disagreed. She reasoned that since love was so scarce every bit was precious.

She had noticed that Santosh had a steady hand, that great detailing went into his paintings, so she asked Jyoti about enrolling him in a pottery class to give him a financially viable skill. She offered to pay the fees for a special class, preferably at a recognised institute.

'After so many months you haven't understood the first thing about these kids, Theresa,' retorted Jyoti, her dark eyes flashing impatiently. 'What makes you think Santosh will attend class regularly? How will other kids treat him when they discover he doesn't have a home? Won't their taunts depress him?'

'If pottery class isn't a good idea what can I do for Santosh?'

'Anything you do for an individual is meaningless. We have to change the system. That's the only solution.'

6 **midriff** middle part of the body – 7 **choli** short blouse worn with a sari – 8 **to acknowledge** to agree or concede that sth is true – 8 **bond** strong connection – 15 **to resent** to feel angry or envious about sth – 16 **to abuse** *here:* to speak cruelly to – 20 **scarce** in short supply – 20 **precious** ['preʃəs] very valuable – 23 **to enrol** to register – 23 **pottery** art of making things (tableware, vases, etc.) from clay – 23 **viable** useful – 24 **fee** price for a service – 27 **to retort** to reply angrily or sharply – 30 **taunt** sth said to mock or hurt sb

'That'll take centuries! Meanwhile lives have to be led. Maybe I can help improve just one life?'

'I'm beginning to agree with your Parsi friends. You are a sentimentalist.'

'Are you also going to say one child more or less makes no difference?'

'Of course not. But you can do more by creating awareness about these kids in the west than by handing out dole to one poor kid.'

'I'll be doing the awareness bit as part of my project anyway. But that shouldn't stop me from doing something special for Santosh.'

'What makes Santosh special? How is he different from the other kids at the shelter? Only the fact that he speaks English. To single him out for special treatment would affect other kids without necessarily benefiting him.

'I feel awful abandoning him.'

'I've been telling you to keep your distance. Emotionally. Now you're going to experience withdrawal pains like he will.'

'It's not just the parting, Jyoti. I want to do something to improve his life.'

'You can't. I only hope you haven't destroyed his survival capacity.'

Reflecting on Jyoti's words depressed Theresa as she chewed on her toast. Her eyes fell on a line of amber-coloured ants labouring up the windowsill with crumbs of her breakfast. Every crumb is precious to someone, she thought, wondering whether Santosh would be nibbled up bit by bit or find the ingenuity to survive.

The contrast between the high-flying lifestyle of Cawas' friends and the streetkids among whom she spent her days deepened Theresa's understanding of India, though she realised there was more to the country than monuments, slums and an urban elite. The common thread running through her

8 **dole** money given to a poor person – 15 **to single sb/sth out** to pick out as special – 16 **to benefit** to be good for – 17 **to abandon** to leave behind (and not care for any more) – 23 **capacity** *here:* ability – 25 **amber** dark yellow, like the semi-precious jewel (*Bernstein*) – 28 **to nibble** to eat away in small bites – 29 **ingenuity** [ˌɪndʒɪˈnjuːɪtɪ] cleverness, ability to find solutions to problems – 34 **common thread** what both had in common, i.e. was an element in both

experiences was unpunctuality and with the precision bred in her German character this disturbed her more than the poverty or dirt. Because it seemed easier to correct.

It wasn't just trains and flights that were not on time. It was the people themselves. Ten-fifteen minutes weren't considered much of a delay whereas in Germany a two minute delay in the arrival of a bus would have half the queue stamping in impatience while a person being habitually late by a quarter of an hour would strain friendships.

Here, no one thought Savak unpunctual when he'd arrive to pick her up at eight-fifteen or eight-twenty after telling her to be ready by eight. Jyoti thought nothing of arriving at the shelter at ten-forty-five or eleven a.m. when her scheduled time was ten-thirty. In the early weeks when Theresa was being taken through the guts and grime of the city she would find herself waiting at V. T. station or Chowpatty beach wondering whether she was at the right pre-arranged spot to find Jyoti sauntering up twenty minutes later without so much as an explanation. When they got to know each other better she raised the issue.

'Why does no one respect time in India? You're always late by fifteen-twenty minutes.'

'It's the traffic, the trains. You have to make allowances.'

'If I can reach on time, why can't you?'

'Relax, yaar. Why are you getting neurotic! Five-ten minutes here or there makes no difference!'

'Sometimes I'm waiting in the street. In the hot sun.'

'Sorry … !'

'I'm not complaining. There's so much happening in the streets I can watch it for hours. But there's an ethic of valuing time.'

'As long as work gets done what difference do a few minutes make!'

'Time has to be valued for itself. Apart from work, time for leisure and pleasure is also valuable. One's own time as well as other people's. Time wasted is time lost. Once lost it can never be recovered.'

1 **unpunctuality** not being on time – 1 **to breed, bred** *here:* to become part of one's culture and upbringing – 7 **to stamp** *here:* to walk about angrily and noisily – 8 **habitually** very often, as a general habit – 9 **to strain** to put stress on, make difficult – 15 **guts** *here:* mess, dirt – 16 **V.T.** = Victoria Terminus – 17 **to saunter** to walk slowly and casually – 19 **to raise an issue** to bring up a subject – 22 **to make allowances** to be tolerant because of special circumstances – 24 **yaar** (*Ind.E/Hindi*) friend, pal – 33 **leisure** free time activities – 35 **to recover** to get back

'You're getting philosophical. We only think of practicalities.'

Savak was more apologetic, acknowledging she had reason to feel miffed. 'Sorry but every traffic light was against me,' he would say by way of an explanation. Or 'Just as I was leaving the office the boss called. Luckily I didn't have to cancel our evening.' Occasionally when he did arrive on time there would be triumph in his voice as if he had accomplished something special rather than conformed to a norm. 'I made it on German time today,' he would beam, looking as if he deserved a medal for this feat.

On Theresa's last evening Savak threw a farewell party for her. The previous day he had given her a raw silk outfit with a skirt and softly scalloped blouse. As she drew her head through the neckline and smoothed the fabric over her hips she looked into the mirror to find the rust silk a perfect match for her hair, a colour she had never worn. She couldn't decide whether it suited her or made her look like a ripe tomato.

Zenia complimented her as she emerged from her room and they went down to the car where Cawas was waiting. He drove slowly towards the traffic light knowing it would stay red for they were moving in the opposite direction of the rush hour crowds fleeing the city each night. They stopped, almost touching the bumper of the car ahead when Theresa heard a tapping at her window.

'Santosh! What are you doing here at this time!' The boy was sobbing and jabbering in a language she could not understand. She stepped out to have the child fling his arms around her for the first time since they met. 'My new clothes!' she squealed as Cawas yelled at Santosh from the car. Just then the lights changed and the cars behind them started hooting.

'Get inside!' screamed Zenia but Theresa could not extricate herself from Santosh's flailing arms.

'Carry on. I'll join you later,' she called as impatient drivers hurled abuses at Cawas afraid the short-time signal would change again. Holding Santosh firmly by the wrist she led him to the pavement but his hysteria did not abate. The parting

3 **miffed** (*inf*) upset, annoyed – 7 **to accomplish** to achieve, to manage to do – 8 **to conform to** to act in agreement with – 9 **to beam** *here:* to smile broadly – 9 **feat** great deed – 10 **farewell** goodbye – 11 **outfit** suit of clothes – 12 **scalloped** with several curves at the edge, like a certain shellfish (*Kamm-Muschel*) – 13 **to smooth** to make flat – 17 **to emerge** to come out – 24 **to sob** to cry silently, with gasps of breath – 26 **to squeal** to make a high-pitched sound – 28 **to hoot** *here:* to sound their horns – 29 **to extricate os** to get os out of sth – 30 **to flail** to wave around wildly – 32 **to hurl** to throw; *here:* to express strongly – 34 **to abate** to get weaker

pangs have started, I should have listened to Jyoti, she thought. Through the maze of jumbled words she picked up three names. Raju. Mohan. Shafique. With a start she realised something had happened between Santosh and the three bullies of the shelter.

'Calm down, Santosh. Tell me slowly in English what happened.'

'Didi ... didi ... Raju ... Mohan ... Shafique ....'

'They beat you up. Are you hurt?'

'More bad than beat, didi ... More bad ... They no like you give me ice cream biscuit. Many days they say we teach you good when firang memsahib leave. Two-three time I give them biscuit. They want ice cream. How I can keep ice cream till night? Five-six time they beat me. Leg, hand, head. I keep quiet. Tomorrow you leave Germany, I think I leave shelter. But Raju ... Raju catch me today ...' and his voice trailed off in a fresh round of incoherent babbling.

Cawas had parked the car and crossed over. 'Stop harassing the lady!' he roared but Theresa put her arm protectively around Santosh forgetting about her dress.

'He's been through a traumatic experience. I can't follow the language. Will you please interpret?'

Cawas looked peeved. 'We're getting late for the party.'

'This is an emergency. Please translate.'

'I'll try,' said Cawas reluctantly, not wanting to admit his Hindi wasn't good enough.

'What did Raju do?' she asked Santosh. His lower lip trembled but he remained silent in front of this aggressive stranger. 'I've never seen him like this in the six months I've known him, she told the disgruntled Cawas.

'He's acting. Trying to get money out of you.'

She dismissed his jaundiced thought pattern, her mind sifting through the information she'd gathered over months, trying to

1 **pang** pain – 2 **maze** complicated system of paths, meant to confuse *(here fig)* – 2 **jumbled** mixed up – 11 **firang** (*Hindi*) foreign – 16 **incoherent** hard to understand – 17 **to harass** to deliberately annoy or cause trouble for – 22 **peeved** (*inf*) annoyed – 24 **reluctantly** unwilling – 24 **Hindi** Santosh may have spoken a language unknown to Cawas: Though Gujarati is the native language of most Parsis, they would also be fluent in the official language Hindi, and the local language Marathi as well as English. – 26 **to tremble** to shake slightly – 29 **disgruntled** very annoyed – 31 **jaundiced** prejudiced (from the kidney disease jaundice (*Gelbsucht*), which affects the skin and the mind) – 31 **to sift** to search through

guess what might have gone wrong. 'Did Raju do something which you can't say in English?' she asked the disturbed boy.

He nodded, his terror-stricken eyes fixed on her face. 'Did Raju rape you?'

He looked uncomprehending. She turned to Cawas. 'Ask him if he's been raped.'

'What!'

'Ask him if he's been raped by Raju.'

'Have you gone crazy! Do you think I'd talk about such intimate matters to a stranger! That too a beggar-child!' retorted an incredulous Cawas.

'Rape is not intimate!'

'Stop wasting time, Theresa. Come to the car. Everybody's waiting. It's your farewell party.'

'I can't leave till I know what's happened to Santosh.'

'Look. The traffic cop's got after Zenia.'

'You carry on. I'll take a cab and join you later.'

'Stop being stubborn, Theresa! Savak's waiting for you.'

'I said I'll come later.' She turned back to Santosh leading him towards the low wall along the seafront. They stood leaning against it and talked in low voices. 'Sex,' suddenly the word came to him. 'Raju sex me. From back. After Raju, Mohan. After Mohan, Shafique.'

'Wasn't anyone around?'

'Raju call me to garden. Behind Jyoti-madam office. I no go. Raju-Shafique catch left-hand, right-hand. Take me jabardasti. First they beat me. Hand, leg, back, front. Like before. Then they talk about you. Firang memsahib have white-white skin. Firang memsahib have big-big watermelons. Then they pull shorts. Shafique hold, Raju go inside. Again, again, again. Then Raju hold Mohan go inside. All time I am screaming-crying. No one comes. Now they say they will do every day. I leave Bombay, didi. I take night train.'

'Calm down Santosh. We must report this to Jyoti.'

'You report, didi. I go. I report ... they kill me.'

'You have to report this, Santosh. Those boys will rape others.'

4 **to rape** to force a sexual act on – 5 **uncomprehending** not understanding – 11 **incredulous** [ɪn'kredjʊləs] not believing – 18 **stubborn** ['stʌbən] very determined, hard to persuade – 26 **jabardasti** (*vulg*) word used in several Indian languages to refer to rape

'You report ... I go ... I go to station now ...'

'Where will you go?'

'Anywhere ... first train ... anywhere ...'

'Just wait till I phone Jyoti ...'

'You tell Jyoti Madam, didi ... I go ... Salaam. Goodbye. Bye-bye.'

And he disappeared into the dark, weaving his way through the orange-red tail lights of the crawling traffic. Theresa stayed by the sea for a long while, trying to collect her thoughts. When she managed to reach Savak's place she was met with icy stares.

'I hope she doesn't have AIDS. She might infect us!' she heard the fat woman remarking loud enough for her to hear.

5 **salaam** Muslim greeting meaning 'peace', also used in Indian languages – 8 **to crawl** *here:* to move very slowly

Salman Rushdie

About the Author

Salman Rushdie is the author of nine novels, one collection of short stories, and four works of nonfiction, and the co-editor of The Vantage Book of Indian Writing. In 1993 *Midnight's Children* was judged to be the 'Booker of Bookers', the best novel to have won the Booker Prize in its first 25 years.

The Moor's Last Sigh won the Whitbread Prize in 1995, and the European Union's Aristeion Prize for Literature in 1996. In 2007 he was awarded a Knighthood for services to literature. He is a Fellow of the Royal Society of Literature and a Commandeur des Arts et des Lettres.

Salman Rushdie

Good Advice is Rarer than Rubies

On the last Tuesday of the month, the dawn bus, its headlamps still shining, brought Miss Rehana to the gates of the British Consulate. It arrived pushing a cloud of dust, veiling her beauty from the eyes of strangers until she descended. The bus was brightly painted in multicoloured arabesques, and on the front it said 'MOVE OVER DARLING' in green and gold letters; on the back it added 'TATA-BATA' and also 'O.K. GOOD-LIFE'. Miss Rehana told the driver it was a beautiful bus, and he jumped down and held the door open for her, bowing theatrically as she descended.

Miss Rehana's eyes were large and black and bright enough not to need the help of antimony, and when the advice expert Muhammad Ali saw them he felt himself becoming young again. He watched her approaching the Consulate gates as the light strengthened, and asking the bearded lala who guarded them in a gold-buttoned khaki uniform with a cockaded turban when they would open. The lala, usually so rude to the Consulate's Tuesday women, answered Miss Rehana with something like courtesy.

"Half an hour," he said gruffly. "Maybe two hours. Who knows? The sahibs are eating their breakfast."

The dusty compound between the bus stop and the Consulate was already full of Tuesday women, some veiled, a few barefaced like Miss Rehana. They all looked frightened, and leaned heavily on the arms of uncles or brothers, who were trying to look confident. But Miss Rehana had come on her own, and did not seem at all alarmed.

ruby a red jewel – 1 **dawn** early morning – 3 **to veil** *here:* to hide – 5 **arabesque** design of flowing lines – 7 **TATA-BATA** two well-known Indian companies – 12 **antimony** [□n'tɪmənɪ] silvery make-up which makes the eyes shine – 15 **lala** *(Hindi)* watchman – 16 **cockaded** decorated with a feather or ribbon – 19 **courtesy** ['kɜ:tɪsɪ] politeness – 20 **gruffly** abruptly – 21 **sahib** *(Hindi)* term of respect for a man – 22 **compound** building(s) surrounded by a wall – 23 **barefaced** the face not being covered by a veil

Muhammad Ali, who specialised in advising the most vulnerable-looking of these weekly supplicants, found his feet leading him towards the strange, big-eyed, independent girl.

"Miss," he began. "You have come for permit to London, I think so?"

She was standing at a hot-snack stall in the little shanty-town by the edge of the compound, munching chilli-pakoras contentedly. She turned to look at him, and at close range those eyes did bad things to his digestive tract.

"Yes, I have."

"Then, please, you allow me to give some advice? Small cost only."

Miss Rehana smiled. "Good advice is rarer than rubies," she said. "But alas, I cannot pay. I am an orphan, not one of your wealthy ladies."

"Trust my grey hairs," Muhammad Ali urged her. "My advice is well tempered by experience. You will certainly find it good."

She shook her head. "I tell you I am a poor potato. There are women here with male family members, all earning good wages. Go to them. Good advice should find good money."

I am going crazy, Muhammad Ali thought, because he heard his voice telling her of its own volition, "Miss, I have been drawn to you by Fate. What to do? Our meeting was written. I also am a poor man only, but for you my advice comes free."

She smiled again. "Then I must surely listen. When Fate sends a gift, one receives good fortune."

He led her to the low wooden desk in his own special corner of the shanty-town. She followed, continuing to eat pakoras from a little newspaper packet. She did not offer him any.

Muhammad Ali put a cushion on the dusty ground. "Please to sit." She did as he asked. He sat cross-legged across the desk from her, conscious that two or three dozen pairs of male eyes

2 **supplicant** *(form)* sb in an inferior position asking for sth – 4 **permit** official document giving the right to do sth – 6 **stall** table in the open air used for selling sth – 6 **shanty-town** slum – 7 **to munch** to eat steadily – 7 **pakora** *Indian snack (*deep-fried piece of vegetable, chicken, etc. served with a spicy sauce) – 8 **at close range** at a short distance – 9 **digestive tract** *here:* stomach – 14 **orphan** a child whose parents are both dead – 17 **well tempered** *here:* supported – 22 **of its own volition** as if it has a will of its own – 24 **to come free** to cost nothing – 25 **fate** what must happen *(Schicksal)*

were watching him enviously, that all the other shanty-town men were ogling the latest young lovely to be charmed by the old grey-hair fraud. He took a deep breath to settle himself.

"Name, please."

"Miss Rehana," she told him. "Fiancée of Mustafa Dar of Bradford, London."

"Bradford, England," he corrected her gently. "London is a town only, like Multan or Bahawalpur. England is a great nation full of the coldest fish in the world."

"I see. Thank you," she responded gravely, so that he was unsure if she was making fun of him.

"You have filled application form? Then let me see, please."

She passed him a neatly folded document in a brown envelope.

"Is it OK?" For the first time there was a note of anxiety in her voice.

He patted the desk quite near the place where her hand rested. "I am certain," he said. "Wait on and I will check."

She finished the pakoras while he scanned her papers.

"Tip-top," he pronounced at length. "All in order."

"Thank you for your advice," she said, making as if to rise. "I'll go now and wait by the gate."

"What are your thinking?" he cried loudly, smiting his forehead. "You consider this is easy business? Just give the form and proof, with a big smile they hand over the permit? Miss Rehana, I tell you, you are entering a worse place than any police station."

"Is it so, truly?" His oratory had done the trick. She was a captive audience now, and he would be able to look at her for a few moments longer.

Drawing another calming breath, he launched into his set speech. He told her that the sahibs thought that all the women

2 **to ogle** to stare at sb in a way that shows sexual interest – 3 **fraud** sb who lies and pretends to be able to do sth – 3 **to settle os** to become calm – 5 **fiancée** woman who has promised to marry sb – 6 **Bradford** industrial city in the north of England – 8 **Multan, Bahawalpur** cities in Pakistan – 10 **gravely** very seriously – 13 **neatly** tidily, carefully – 15 **anxiety** [□ŋg'zaɪətɪ] worry – 17 **to pat** to touch gently and repeatedly – 19 **to scan** to look through – 23 **to smite, smote, smitten** *(old use)* to hit – 28 **oratory** *(form)* power of a speech – 29 **captive audience** sb who has to listen to sb else – 31 **to launch into sth** to begin sth

who came on Tuesdays, claiming to be dependents of bus drivers in Luton or chartered accountants in Manchester, were crooks and liars and cheats.

She protested, "But then I will simply tell them that I, for one, am no such thing!"

Her innocence made him shiver with fear for her. She was a sparrow, he told her, and they were men with hooded eyes, like hawks. He explained that they would ask her questions, personal questions, questions such as a lady's own brother would be too shy to ask. They would ask if she was virgin, and, if not, what her fiancé's love-making habits were, and what secret nicknames they had invented for one another.

Muhammad Ali spoke brutally, on purpose, to lessen the shock she would feel when it, or something like it, actually happened. Her eyes remained steady, but her hands began to flutter at the edges of the desk.

He went on:

"They will ask you how many rooms are in your family home, and what colour are the walls, and what days do you empty the rubbish. They will ask your man's mother's third cousin's aunt's step-daughter's middle name. And all these things they have already asked your Mustafa Dar in his Bradford. And if you make one mistake, you are finished."

"Yes," she said, and he could hear her disciplining her voice. "And what is your advice, old man?"

It was at this point that Muhammad Ali usually began to whisper urgently, to mention that he knew a man, a very good type, who worked in the Consulate, and through him, for a fee, the necessary papers could be delivered, with all the proper authenticating seals. Business was good, because the women would often pay him five hundred rupees or give him a gold bracelet for his pains, and go away happy.

1 **dependent** sb who is supported financially by sb else – 2 **Luton** town in England – 2 **chartered accountant** *staatlich geprüfter Bilanzbuchhalter* – 3 **crook** *(inf)* dishonest person – 6 **to shiver** to shake – 7 **sparrow** *Spatz* – 7 **hooded** *here:* with partly closed eyes – 8 **hawk** *Falke* – 10 **virgin** woman/girl who has not yet had sex – 12 **nickname** a shortened, informal version of a name – 16 **to flutter** to move nervously – 29 **to deliver** to hand over – 30 **authenticating** making sth legal – 30 **seal** official mark to show that documents are legal – 31 **rupee** Indian currency unit

They came from hundreds of miles away – he normally made sure of this before beginning to trick them – so even when they discovered they had been swindled they were unlikely to return. They went away to Sargodha or Lalukhet and began to pack, and who knows at what point they found out they had been gulled, but it was at a too-late point, anyway.

Life is hard, and an old man must live by his wits. It was not up to Muhammad Ali to have compassion for these Tuesday women.

But once again his voice betrayed him, and instead of starting his customary speech it began to reveal to her his greatest secret.

"Miss Rehana," his voice said, and he listened to it in amazement, "you are a rare person, a jewel, and for you I will do what I would not do for my own daughter, perhaps. One document has come into my possession that can solve all your worries at one stroke."

"And what is this sorcerer's paper?" she asked, her eyes unquestion-ably laughing at him now.

His voice fell low-as-low.

"Miss Rehana, it is a British passport. Completely genuine and pukka goods. I have a good friend who will put your name and photo, and then, hey-presto, England there you come!"

He had said it!

Anything was possible now, on this day of his insanity. Probably he would give her the thing free-gratis, and then kick himself for a year afterwards.

Old fool, he berated himself. The oldest fools are *bewitch*ed by the youngest girls.

"Let me understand you," she was saying. "You are proposing I should commit a crime…"

4 **Sargodha** city in Northeast Pakistan – 4 **Lalukhet** suburb of Karachi, South Pakistan – 6 **to gull** *(old use)* to fool – 7 **to live by one's wits** to earn money by clever tricks – 8 **compassion** pity – 10 **to betray** *here:* to do sth one does not want – 11 **customary** usual – 11 **to reveal** *here:* to tell – 17 **at one stroke** at once – 18 **sorcerer** magician – 20 **to fall low-as-low** to become quiet – 22 **pukka** *(Hindi)* authentic – 25 **insanity** madness – 28 **to berate** to criticize angrily – 28 **to bewitch** to charm as if by magic

"Not crime," he interposed. "Facilitation."

"... and go to Bradford, London, illegally, and therefore justify the low opinion the Consulate sahibs have of us all. Old babuji, this is not good advice."

"Bradford, *England*," he corrected her mournfully. "You should not take my gift in such a spirit."

"Then how?"

"Bibi, I am a poor fellow, and I have offered this prize because you are so beautiful. Do not spit on my generosity. Take the thing. Or else don't take, go home, forget England, only do not go into that building and lose your dignity."

But she was on her feet, turning away from him, walking towards the gates, where the women had begun to cluster and the lala was swearing at them to be patient or none of them would be admitted at all.

"So be a fool," Muhammad Ali shouted after her. "What goes of my father's if you are?" (Meaning, what was it to him.)

She did not turn.

"It is the curse of our people," he yelled. "We are poor, we are ignorant, and we completely refuse to learn."

"Hey, Muhammad Ali," the woman at the betel-nut stall called across to him. "Too bad, she likes them young."

That day Muhammad Ali did nothing but stand around near the Consulate gates. Many times he scolded himself, *Go from here, old goof, lady does not desire to speak with you any further*. But when she came out, she found him waiting.

"Salaam, advice wallah," she greeted him.

She seemed calm, and at peace with him again, and he thought, My God, ya Allah, she has *pulled it off*. The British sahibs also have been *drown*ing in her eyes and she has got her passage to England.

1 **to interpose** *(form)* to interrupt with a comment – 1 **facilitation** act of making sth easier – 3 **babuji** *(Hindi, Urdu) (literally)* dear father; respectful form of address for an older person – 5 **mournfully** sadly – 9 **to spit on** *(here fig)* to show disrespect – 11 **dignity** self-respect – 13 **to cluster** to gather – 19 **curse** *here:* sth that causes problems – 21 **betel** ['bi:təl] plant that produces nuts and leaves with a midly narcotic effect – 24 **to scold os** to find fault with os – 25 **goof** *(inf)* stupid person – 27 **salaam** *(Arabic)* Urdu Muslim greeting accompanied by a deep bow with the right hand on the forehead – 27 **wallah** *(Ind.E)* person responsible for sth, e.g. the "advice wallah" gives advice – 29 **to pull sth off** to succeed in doing sth – 30 **to drown in sb's eyes** to be overpowered by sb's attractiveness

He smiled at her hopefully. She smiled back with no trouble at all.

"Miss Rehana Begum," he said, "felicitations, daughter, on what is obviously your hour of triumph."

Impulsively, she took his forearm in her hand.

"Come," she said. "Let me buy you a pakora to thank you for your advice and to apologise for my rudeness, too."

They stood in the dust of the afternoon compound near the bus, which was getting ready to leave. Coolies were tying bedding rolls to the roof. A hawker shouted at the passengers, trying to sell them love stories and green medicines, both of which cured unhappiness. Miss Rehana and a happy Muhammad Ali ate their pakoras sitting on the bus's 'front mud-guard', that is, the bumper. The old advice expert began softly to hum a tune from a movie soundtrack. The day's heat was gone.

"It was an arranged engagement," Miss Rehana said all at once. "I was nine years old when my parents fixed it. Mustafa Dar was already thirty at that time, but my father wanted someone who could look after me as he had done himself and Mustafa was a man known to Daddyji as a solid type. Then my parents died and Mustafa Dar went to England and said he would send for me. That was many years ago. I have his photo, but he is like a stranger to me. Even his voice, I do not recognize it on the phone."

The confession took Muhammad Ali by surprise, but he nodded with what he hoped looked like wisdom.

"Still and after all," he said, "one's parents act in one's best interests. They found you a good and honest man who has kept his word and sent for you. And now you have a lifetime to get to know him, and to love."

3 **begum** *(Hindi)* polite form of address for a woman – 3 **felicitations** congratulations – 9 **coolie** a cheaply hired, unskilled, Oriental labourer – 10 **hawker** man who sells goods in the street – 13 **mud-guard** piece of metal over the wheels which protects them from water and dirt – 14 **bumper** *Stoßstange* – 16 **arranged engagement** a planned marriage in which the parents choose a partner for their child – 25 **confession** *here:* telling personal things – 26 **wisdom** sensible understanding

He was puzzled, now, by the bitterness that had infected her smile.

"But, old man," she asked him, "why have you already packed me and posted me off to England?"

He stood up, shocked.

"You looked happy – so I just assumed ... excuse me, but they turned you down or what?"

"I got all their questions wrong," she replied. "Distinguishing marks I put on the wrong cheeks, bathroom décor I completely redecorated, all absolutely topsy-turvy, you see."

"But what to do? How will you go?"

"Now I will go back to Lahore and my job. I work in a great house, as ayah to three good boys. They would have been sad to see me leave."

"But this is tragedy!" Muhammad Ali lamented. "Oh, how I pray that you had taken up my offer! Now, but, it is not possible, I regret to inform. Now they have your form on file, cross-check can be made, even the passport will not suffice."

"It is spoilt, all spoilt, and it could have been so easy if advice had been accepted in good time."

"I do not think," she told him, "I truly do not think you should be sad."

Her last smile, which he watched from the compound until the bus concealed it in a dust-cloud, was the happiest thing he had ever seen in his long, hot, hard, unloving life.

1 **puzzled** confused – 1 **to infect** *here:* to spoil – 8 **distinguishing mark** special characteristic – 10 **topsy-turvy** *(inf)* upside down – 12 **Lahore** city in Northeast Pakistan – 13 **ayah** *(Hindi)* a nanny – 15 **to lament** to express sorrow – 17 **cross-check** making sure sth is correct by comparing it with sth else – 18 **to suffice** to be enough – 24 **to conceal** to hide

Salman Rushdie

The Free Radio

We all knew nothing good would happen to him while the thief's widow had her claws dug into his flesh, but the boy was an innocent, a real donkey's child, you can't teach such people.

That boy could have had a good life. God had blessed him with God's own looks, and his father had gone to the grave for him, but didn't he leave the boy a brandnew first-class cycle rickshaw with plastic covered seats and all? So: looks he had, his own trade he had, there would have been a good wife in time, he should just have taken out some years to save some rupees; but no, he must fall for a thief's widow before the hairs had time to come out on his chin, before his milk-teeth had split, one might say.

We felt bad for him, but who listens to the wisdom of the old today?

I say: who listens?

Exactly, nobody, certainly not a stone-head like Ramani the rickshaw-wallah. But I blame the widow. I saw it happen, you know, I saw most of it until I couldn't stand any more. I sat under this very banyan, smoking this selfsame hookah, and not much escaped my notice.

And at one time I tried to save him from his fate, but it was no go …

The widow was certainly attractive, no point denying, in a sort of hard vicious way she was all right, but it is her mentality that was rotten. Ten years older than Ramani she must have been, five children alive and two dead, what that thief did besides robbing and making babies God only knows, but he left her not one new paisa, so of course she would be interested in Ramani. I'm not saying a rickshaw-wallah makes much in this town but

2 **widow** woman whose husband is dead – 2 **claws** pointed ends of birds feet (*here fig*) – 3 **innocent** *here:* naïve, simple-minded – 6 **cycle rickshaw** ['rɪkʃɔː] tricycle with seat for passengers, used as a taxi – 8 **trade** *here:* business, job – 9 **rupee** Indian currency unit – 11 **to split, split, split** *here:* to grow, come out – 17 **wallah** (*Ind.E*) person responsible for sth – 19 **banyan** tropical tree – 19 **hookah** water pipe – 21 **fate** what must happen (*Schicksal*) – 22 **no go** (*inf*) not possible – 24 **vicious** hateful and cruel – 25 **rotton** gone bad – 28 **paisa** ['peisə] Indian coin worth one hundredth of a rupee

two mouthfuls are better to eat than wind. And not many people will look twice at the widow of a good-for-nothing.

They met right here.

One day Ramani rode into town without a passenger, but grinning as usual as if someone had given him a ten-chip tip, singing some playback music from the radio, his hair greased like for a wedding. He was not such a fool that he didn't know how the girls watched him all the time and passed remarks about his long and well-muscled legs.

The thief's widow had gone to the bania shop to buy some three grains of dal and I won't say where the money came from, but people saw men at night near her rutputty shack, even the bania himself they were telling me but I personally will not comment.

She had all her five brats with her and then and there, cool as a fan, she called out: '*Hey! Rickshaaa!*' Loud, you know, like a truly cheap type. Showing us she can afford to ride in rickshaws, as if anyone was interested. Her children must have gone hungry to pay for the ride but in my opinion it was an investment for her, because must-be she had decided already to put her hooks into Ramani. So they all poured into the rickshaw and he took her away, and with the five kiddies as well as the widow there was quite a weight, so he was puffing hard, and the veins were standing out on his legs, and I thought, careful, my son, or you will have this burden to pull for all of your life.

But after that Ramani and the thief's widow were seen everywhere, shamelessly, in public places, and I was glad his mother was dead because if she had lived to see this her face would have fallen off from shame.

Sometimes in those days Ramani came into this street in the evenings to meet some friends, and they thought they were very smart because they would go into the back room of the Irani's canteen and drink illegal liquor, only of course everybody knew, but who would do anything, if boys ruin their lives let their relations worry.

5 **chip** *here:* coin – 6 **greased** oiled – 10 **bania** (*Urdu*) grocer('s) – 11 **dal** (*Hindi/Urdu*) lentils (*Linsen*) – 12 **rutputty** (*Ind.E slang*) shabby and messy – 12 **shack** roughly built hut – 15 **brat** (*inf, derog*) badly-behaved child – 16 **fan** machine or object which moves to cool the air – 23 **to puff** to breathe heavily – 33 **liquor** ['lɪkə] strong alcoholic drink

I was sad to see Ramani fall into this bad company. His parents were known to me when alive. But when I told Ramani to keep away from those hot-shots he grinned like a sheep and said I was wrong, nothing bad was taking place.

Let it go, I thought.

I knew those cronies of his. They all wore the armbands of the new Youth Movement. This was the time of the State of Emergency, and these friends were not peaceful persons, there were stories of beatings-up, so I sat quiet under my tree. Ramani wore no armband but he went with them because they impressed him, the fool.

These armband youths were always flattering Ramani. Such a handsome chap, they told him, compared to you Shashi Kapoor and Amitabh are like lepers only, you should go to Bombay and be put in the motion pictures.

They flattered him with dreams because they knew they could take money from him at cards and he would buy them drink while they did it, though he was no richer than they. So now Ramani's head became filled with these movie dreams, because there was nothing else inside to take up any space, and this is another reason why I blame the widow woman, because she had more years and should have had more sense. In two ticks she could have made him forget all about it, but no, I heard her telling him one day for all to hear, 'Truly you have the looks of Lord Krishna himself, except you are not blue all over.' In the street! So all would know they were lovers! From that day on I was sure a disaster would happen.

The next time the thief's widow came into the street to visit the bania shop I decided to act. Not for my own sake but for the boy's dead parents I risked being shamed by a … no, I will not call her the name, she is elsewhere now and they will know what she is like.

'Thief's widow!' I called out.

3 **hot-shot** (*inf, sarcastic*) important person – 6 **crony** (*inf, derog*) follower – 6 **armband** cloth worn around upper arm (*Armbinde*) – 7 **State of Emergency** period of authoritarian rule imposed by Prime Minister Indira Gandhi from 1975-1977 – 9 **beating-up** physical attack on sb – 11 **to impress** to generate respect or admiration – 12 **to flatter** to express admiration in an insincere way – 13 **chap** fellow – 13 **Shashi Kapoor, Amitabh (Bachchan)** stars of the Bombay film industry ('Bollywood') – 14 **leper** sb who has leprosy – 23 **ticks** seconds (i.e. very short time) – 25 **Krishna** major Hindu god – 29 **for my own sake** for me

She stopped dead, jerking her face in an ugly way, as if I had hit her with a whip.

'Come here and speak,' I told her.

Now she could not refuse because I am not without importance in the town and maybe she calculated that if people saw us talking they would stop ignoring her when she passed, so she came as I knew she would.

'I have to say this thing only,' I told her with dignity. 'Ramani the rickshaw boy is dear to me, and you must find some person of your own age, or, better still, go to the widows' ashrams in Benares and spend the rest of your life there in holy prayer, thanking God that widow-burning is now illegal.'

So at this point she tried to shame me by screaming out and calling me curses and saying that I was a poisonous old man who should have died years ago, and then she said, 'Let me tell you, mister teacher sahib *retired*, that your Ramani has asked to marry me and I have said no, because I wish no more children, and he is a young man and should have his own. So tell that to the whole world and stop your cobra poison.'

For a time after that I closed my eyes to this affair of Ramani and the thief's widow, because I had done all I could and there were many other things in the town to interest a person like myself. For instance, the local health officer had brought a big white caravan into the street and was given permission to park it out of the way under the banyan tree; and every night men were taken into this van for a while and things were done to them.

I did not care to be in the vicinity at these times, because the youths with armbands were always in attendance, so I took my hookah and sat in another place. I heard rumours of what was happening in the caravan but I closed my ears.

But it was while this caravan, which smelled of ether, was in town that the extent of the widow's wickedness became plain; because at this time Ramani suddenly began to talk about his

1 **to jerk** to make a short, sudden movement – 8 **dignity** manner expressing honour and importance – 10 **ashram** Hindu religious community – 11 **Benares** = Varanasi, city on the river Ganges – 12 **widow-burning** reference to the old Hindu custom of 'sati' (or 'suttee') – 16 **sahib** (*Hindi*) term of respect for a man – 27 **in the vicinity** nearby – 29 **hookah** pipe with long tube and water container for smoking tobacco – 29 **rumour** information passed around by gossip – 31 **ether** ['iːθə] gas used as an anaesthetic – 32 **wickedness** immorality

new fantasy, telling everyone he could find that very shortly he was to receive a highly special and personalised gift from the Central Government in Delhi itself, and this gift was to be a brand-new first-class battery-operated transistor radio.

Now then: we had always believed that our Ramani was a little soft in the head, with his notions of being a film star and what all; so most of us just nodded tolerantly and said, 'Yes, Ram, that is nice for you,' and, 'What a fine, generous Government it is that gives radios to persons who are so keen on popular music.'

But Ramani insisted it was true, and seemed happier than at any time in his life, a happiness which could not be explained simply by the supposed imminence of the transistor.

Soon after the dream-radio was first mentioned, Ramani and the thief's widow were married, and then I understood everything. I did not attend the nuptials – it was a poor affair by all accounts – but not long afterwards I spoke to Ram when he came past the banyan with an empty rickshaw one day.

He came to sit by me and I asked, 'My child, did you go to the caravan? What have you let them do to you?'

'Don't worry,' he replied. 'Everything is tremendously wonderful. I am in love, teacher sahib, and I have made it possible for me to marry my woman.'

I confess I became angry; indeed, I almost wept as I realised that Ramani had gone voluntarily to subject himself to a humiliation which was being forced upon the other men who were taken to the caravan. I reproved him bitterly. 'My idiot child, you have let that woman deprive you of your manhood!'

'It is not so bad,' Ram said, meaning the *nasbandi*. 'It does not stop love-making or anything, excuse me, teacher sahib, for speaking of such a thing. It stops babies only and my woman did not want children any more, so now all is hundred per cent OK. Also it is in national interest,' he pointed out. 'And soon the free radio will arrive.'

'The free radio,' I repeated.

9 **keen on** fond of, interested in – 12 **imminence** *here:* expected arrival – 15 **nuptials** wedding festivities – 25 **humiliation** act which hurts sb's honour or dignity – 26 **to reprove** to scold, express disapproval sb's behaviour – 27 **to deprive of** to take away – 28 **nasbandi** (*Hindi*) sterilization, vasectomy

'Yes, remember, teacher sahib,' Ram said confidentially, 'some years back, in my kiddie days, when Laxman the tailor had this operation? In no time the radio came and from all over town people gathered to listen to it. It is how the Government says thank you. It will be excellent to have.'

'Go away, get away from me,' I cried out in despair, and did not have the heart to tell him what everyone else in the country already knew, which was that the free radio scheme was a dead duck, long gone, long forgotten. It had been over – *funtoosh*! – for years.

After these events the thief's widow, who was now Ram's wife, did not come into town very often, no doubt being too ashamed of what she had made him do, but Ramani worked longer hours than ever before, and every time he saw any of the dozens of people he'd told about the radio he would put one hand up to his ear as if he were already holding the blasted machine in it, and he would mimic broadcasts with a certain energetic skill.

'*Yé Akashvani hai*,' he announced to the streets. 'This is All-India Radio. Here is the news. A Government spokesman today announced that Ramani rickshaw-wallah's radio was on its way and would be delivered at any moment. And now some playback music.' After which he would sing songs by Asha Bhonsle or Lata Mangeshkar in a high, ridiculous falsetto.

Ram always had the rare quality of total belief in his dreams, and there were times when his faith in the imaginary radio almost took us in, so that we half-believed it was really on its way, or even that it was already there, cupped invisibly against his ear as he rode his rickshaw around the streets of the town. We began to expect to hear Ramani, around a corner or at the far end of a lane, ringing his bell and yelling cheerfully:

'All-India Radio! This is All-India Radio!'

---

8 **scheme** [ski:m] plan – 9 **funtoosh** (*Hindi slang*) great fun – 16 **blasted** (*inf, vulg*) swear word (a weakened substitute for 'bloody') – 17 **to mimic** to imitate – 18 **Ye Akashvani hai** (*Hindi*) This is 'Voice from the Sky' (official name for AIR – All-India Radio) – 23 **falsetto** high voice (like a woman's) – 26 **to take sb in** to fool or trick sb – 27 **cupped** held like a cup

Time passed. Ram continued to carry the invisible radio around town. One year passed. Still his caricatures of the radio channel filled the air in the streets. But when I saw him now, there was a new thing in his face, a strained thing, as if he were having to make a phenomenal effort, which was much more tiring than driving a rickshaw, more tiring even than pulling a rickshaw containing a thief's widow and her five living children and the ghosts of two dead ones; as if all the energy of his young body was being poured into that fictional space between his ear and his hand, and he was trying to bring the radio into existence by a mighty, and possibly fatal, act of will.

I felt most helpless, I can tell you, because I had divined that Ram had poured into the idea of the radio all his worries and regrets about what he had done, and that if the dream were to die he would be forced to face the full gravity of his crime against his own body, to understand that the thief's widow had turned him, before she married him, into a thief of a stupid and terrible kind, because she had made him rob himself.

And then the white caravan came back to its place under the banyan tree and I knew there was nothing to be done, because Ram would certainly come to get his gift.

He did not come for one day, then for two, and I learned afterwards that he had not wished to seem greedy; he didn't want the health officer to think he was desperate for the radio. Besides, he was half hoping they would come over and give it to him at his place, perhaps with some kind of small, formal presentation ceremony. A fool is a fool and there is no accounting for his notions.

On the third day he came. Ringing his bicycle-bell and imitating weather forecasts, ear cupped as usual, he arrived at the caravan. And in the rickshaw behind him sat the thief's widow, the witch, who had not been able to resist coming along to watch her companion's destruction.

11 **fatal** ['feɪtl] disastrous, deadly – 12 **to divine** to understand (*usu* by supernatural means) – 15 **gravity** seriousness – 28 **to account for** to explain – 28 **notion** strange or unrealistic idea

It did not take very long.

Ram went into the caravan gaily, waving at his arm-banded cronies who were guarding it against the anger of the people, and I am told – for I had left the scene to spare myself the pain – that his hair was well-oiled and his clothes were freshly starched. The thief's widow did not move from the rickshaw, but sat there with a black sari pulled over her head, clutching at her children as if they were straws.

After a short time there were sounds of disagreement inside the caravan, and then louder noises still, and finally the youths in armbands went in to see what was becoming, and soon after that Ram was frogmarched out by his drinking-chums, and his hair-grease was smudged on to his face and there was blood coming from his mouth. His hand was no longer cupped by his ear.

And still – they tell me – the thief's black widow did not move from her place in the rickshaw, although they dumped her husband in the dust.

Yes, I know, I'm an old man, my ideas are wrinkled with age, and these days they tell me sterilisation and God knows what is necessary, and maybe I'm wrong to blame the widow as well – why not? Maybe all the views of the old can be discounted now, and if that's so, let it be. But I'm telling this story and I haven't finished yet.

Some days after the incident at the caravan I saw Ramani selling his rickshaw to the old Muslim crook who runs the bicycle-repair shop. When he saw me watching, Ram came to me and said, 'Goodbye, teacher sahib, I am off to Bombay, where I will become a bigger film star than Shashi Kapoor or Amitabh Bachchan even.'

' "I am off," you say?' I asked him. 'Are you perhaps travelling alone?'

2 **gaily** cheerfully – 6 **starched** made stiff by treating with starch, then ironed – 7 **clutching ...** allusion to the idiom 'to clutch at straws' (= to grab at straws to save os from drowning, i.e. to hold an unrealistic hope) – 12 **to frogmarch** (*inf*) to force sb to walk by holding his arms back – 13 **smudged** spread to make sth dirty – 17 **to dump** to throw away (like rubbish) – 19 **wrinkled** (*of skin*) with lines and furrows (*here fig*) – 22 **to discount** [dɪsˈkaʊnt] to pay no attention to, disregard – 26 **crook** [krʊk] (*inf*) dishonest person; criminal, thief

He stiffened. The thief's widow had already taught him not to be humble in the presence of elders.

'My wife and children will come also,' he said. It was the last time we spoke. They left that same day on the down train.

After some months had passed I got his first letter, which was not written by himself, of course, since in spite of all my long-ago efforts he barely knew how to write. He had paid a professional letter-writer, which must have cost him many rupees, because everything in life costs money and in Bombay it costs twice as much. Don't ask me why he wrote to me, but he did. I have the letters and can give you proof positive, so maybe there are some uses for old people still, or maybe he knew I was the only one who would be interested in his news.

Anyhow: the letters were full of his new career, they told me how he'd been discovered at once, a big studio had given him a test, now they were grooming him for stardom, he spent his days at the Sun'n'Sand Hotel at Juhu beach in the company of top lady artistes, he was buying a big house at Pali Hill, built in the split-level mode and incorporating the latest security equipment to protect him from the movie fans, the thief's widow was well and happy and getting fat, and life was filled with light and success and no-questions-asked alcohol.

They were wonderful letters, brimming with confidence, but whenever I read them, and sometimes I read them still, I remember the expression which came over his face in the days just before he learned the truth about his radio, and the huge mad energy which he had poured into the act of conjuring reality, by an act of magnificent faith, out of the hot thin air between his cupped hand and his ear.

1 **to stiffen** *here:* to stand straight and rigid – 2 **humble** feeling or showing that one is inferior – 16 **to groom for stardom** to prepare to become a star (e.g. by improving appearance, skills, etc.) – 17 **Juhu** beach just north of Bombay/Mumbai – 18 **Pali Hill** exclusive residential area – 19 **split-level** with floors partially raised between storeys – 19 **to incorporate** to include as an essential part – 23 **to brim with** to be full to overflowing with – 27 **to conjure** [ˈkʌndʒə] to create by (seeming) magic – 28 **faith** strong belief

Bharati Mukherjee

About the Author

Bharati Mukherjee was born in Calcutta in 1940, into a Hindu Brahmin family. Her father owned a prosperous pharmaceuticals company. Bharati's first language was Bengali, and she learned English when she travelled with her family in Europe for a few years from the age of eight. She studied at the Universities of Calcutta and Baroda, where she received a B.A. in English and an M.A. in Ancient Indian Culture respectively. She then went to the USA to attend the Iowa Writers' Workshop, and earned a PhD in Comparative Literature from the University of Iowa.

Her father had allowed her to travel on the understanding that she would return to an arranged marriage and traditional life in India, but this was not to be. Having married Canadian author Clark Blaise in 1963, Bharati moved to Canada and became a Canadian citizen in 1972. However, she experienced considerable prejudice there against non-European immigrants, and returned to the United States with her family. They have two sons.

She collaborated with her husband on two works of non-fiction, *Days and Nights in Calcutta* (1977), and *The Haunting Legacy of the Air India Tragedy* (1987), relating to the terrorist attack which brought a plane down off the coast of Ireland with great loss of life. She also published two books on Indian politics and society (1991, 1992).

Otherwise she has concentrated on writing fiction. One of her main topics is that of American identity, and whether it can exist in a multi-ethnic society. Her novels include *The Tiger's Daughter* (1971), *Jasmine* (1989), and *Desirable Daughters* (2002) – the latter publicized by talk show host Oprah Winfrey (see pp. 91–93). She won the National Book Critics' Circle Award for best fiction for her short story collection *The Middleman and other Stories* (1988). "Nostalgia" was first published in the collection *Darkness* (1985).

Bharati Mukherjee has taught creative writing at Columbia University and New York University, and is currently Professor of English at the University of California at Berkeley. She is a member of the American Academy of Arts and Sciences.

Bharati Mukherjee

Nostalgia

On a cold, snowless evening in December, Dr Manny Patel, a psychiatric resident at a state hospital in Queens, New York, looked through the storefront window of the 'New Taj Mahal' and for the first time in thirteen years felt the papercut-sharp pain of desire. The woman behind the counter was about twenty, twenty-one, with the buttery-gold skin and the round voluptuous bosom of a Bombay film star.

Dr Patel had driven into Manhattan on an impulse. He had put in one of those afternoons at the hospital that made him realize it was only the mysteries of metabolism that kept him from unprofessional outbursts. Mr Horowitz, a three-hundred-and-ninteen-pound readmitted schizophrenic, had convinced himself that he was Noel Coward and demanded respect from the staff. In less than half-an-hour, Mr Horowitz had sung twenty songs, battered a therapy aide's head against a wall, unbuttoned another patient's blouse in order to bite off her nipples, struck a Jamaican nurse across the face and lunged at Dr Patel, calling him in exquisite English, 'Paki scum.' The nurse asked that Mr Horowitz be placed in the seclusion room, and Dr Patel had agreed. The seclusion order had to be reviewed by a doctor every two hours, and Mr Horowitz's order was renewed by Dr Chuong who had come in two hours late for work.

Dr Patel did not like to lock grown men and women in a seven-by-nine room, especially one without padding on its walls. Mr Horowitz had screamed and sung for almost six hours. Dr Patel had increased his dosage of Haldol. Mr Horowitz was

2 **resident** *here:* doctor living in the hospital while undergoing specialist training – 2 **Queen's** eastern borough of New York city – 3 **storefront** large front window of a shop – 3 **Taj Mahal** famous mausoleum in Agra, India (*here:* used as name of shop) – 4 **papercut** *here:* like the feeling of one's skin being cut by a paper edge – 7 **voluptuous bosom** large shapely breasts – 10 **metabolism** [meˈt□bəlɪzəm] how the body processes food for growth, energy, etc. (which varies individually) – 11 **outburst** expression of great anger or frustration – 12 **readmitted** taken into hospital a second time – 12 **schizophrenic** [ˌskɪtsəʊˈfrenɪk] sb suffering from a psychotic condition that causes hallucinations – 13 **Noel Coward** (1899-1973) English actor, playwright and composer – 15 **to batter** to beat hard – 15 **aide** assistant – 17 **nipple** pointed end of a breast – 17 **to lunge at** to dive towards – 18 **Paki** (*inf, derog*) short for 'Pakistani' – 18 **scum** dirt floating on a liquid; *here:* used to insult a person – 19 **seclusion room** place where sb is held in solitary confinement – 24 **seven-by-nine** 7 feet x 9 feet – 24 **padding** soft material to prevent injury – 26 **Haldol** trade name of haloperidol, an anti-psychotic medication

at war with himself and there was no truce except through psychopharmacology and Dr Patel was suspicious of the side effects of such cures. The Haldol had calmed the prisoner. Perhaps it was unrealistic to want more.

He was grateful that there were so many helpless, mentally disabled people (crazies, his wife called them) in New York state, and that they afforded him and Dr Chuong and even the Jamaican nurse a nice living. But he resented being called a 'Paki scum.' Not even a sick man like Mr Horowitz had the right to do that.

He had chosen to settle in the US. He was not one for nostalgia; he was not an expatriate but a patriot. His wife, Camille, who had grown up in Camden, New Jersey, did not share his enthusiasm for America, and had made fun of him when he voted for President Reagan. Camille was not a hypocrite; she was a predictable paradox. She could cut him down for wanting to move to a three-hundred-thousand-dollar house with an atrium in the dining hall, and for blowing sixty-two thousand on a red Porsche, while she boycotted South African wines and non-union lettuce. She spent guiltless money at Balducci's and on fitness equipment. So he enjoyed his house, his car, so what? He wanted things. He wanted things for Camille and for their son. He loved his family, and his acquisitiveness was entwined with love.

His son was at Andover, costing nearly twelve thousand dollars a year. When Manny converted the twelve thousand from dollars to rupees. which he often did as he sat in his small, dreary office listening for screams in the hall, the staggering rupee figure reassured him that he had done well in the New World. His son had recently taken to wearing a safety pin

1 **truce** temporary end to fighting – 2 **psychopharmacology** [ˌsaɪkəʊˈfɑ(r)məˈkɒlədʒɪ] the science of treating mental illness with drugs – 6 **disabled** unable to function properly – 7 **to afford** *here:* to give, provide – 8 **to resent** to feel angry or upset about – 12 **expatriate** sb who leaves their own country to live in another – 15 **(Ronald) Reagan** (1911-2002) US actor and politician; President 1981-89 – 15 **hypocrite** [ˈhɪpəkrɪt] insincere person – 16 **predictable** *here:* easy to guess what sb is going to do or say – 16 **to cut sb down** (*inf*) to criticize harshly – 18 **atrium** *here:* central area of a building with a high glass ceiling – 18 **to blow** *here:* to spend unwisely, waste – 20 **guiltless** *here:* not causing a feeling of guilt – 20 **Balducci's** a New York gourmet store – 23 **acquisitiveness** desire to own things – 23 **entwined** tied up, closely connected with – 25 **Andover** renowned boarding school in Andover, Massachussetts – 27 **rupees** Indian currency – 28 **dreary** dull and boring – 28 **staggering** *here:* huge, astonishing in size – 30 **to take to** to start doing (sth new or surprising)

through his left earlobe, but nothing the boy could do would diminish his father's love.

He had come to America because of the boy. Well, not exactly *come*, but stayed when his student visa expired. He had met Camille, a nurse, at a teaching hospital and the boy had come along, all eight pounds and ten ounces of him, one balmy summer midnight. He could always go back to Delhi if he wanted to. He had made enough money to retire to India (the conversion into rupees had made him a millionaire several times over). He had bought a condominium in one of the better development 'colonies' of New Delhi, just in case.

America had been very good to him, no question; but there were things that he had given up. There were some boyhood emotions, for instance, that he could no longer retrieve. He lived with the fear that his father would die before he could free himself from the crazies of New York and go home. He missed his parents, especially his father, but he couldn't explain this loss to Camille. She hated her mother who had worked long hours at Korvette's and brought her up alone. Camille's mother now worked at a K-Mart, even though she didn't need the money desperately. Camille's mother was an obsessive-compulsive but that was no reason to hate her. In fact, Manny got along with her very well and often had to carry notes between her and her daughter.

His father was now in his seventies, a loud, brash man with blackened teeth. He still operated the moviehouse he owned. The old man didn't trust the manager he kept on the payroll. He didn't trust anyone except his blood relatives. All the ushers in the moviehouse were poor cousins. Manny was an only child. His mother had been deemed barren, but at age forty-three, goddess Parvati had worked a miracle and Manny had been born. He should go back to India. He should look after his parents. Out

1 **earlobe** outer part of the ear – 2 **to diminish** to lessen – 4 **to expire** to run out, be no longer valid – 7 **balmy** pleasantly warm – 10 **condominium** apartment which is owned, not rented (*Eigentumswohnung*) – 14 **to retrieve** to get back (*here:* feel again) – 19 **Korvette's** chain of New York discount stores that went out of business in1980 – 20 **K-Mart** chain of US discount stores – 21 **obsessive-compulsive** sb with a mental disorder that makes one feel one has to do certain things repeatedly – 25 **brash** offensively loud – 27 **on the payroll** as a member of the paid staff – 28 **usher** person whose job it is to show people to their seats – 30 **deemed barren** believed to be unable to have children – 31 **Parvati** Hindu goddess personifying certain values, including fertility

of a sense of duty to the goddess, if not out of love for his father. Money, luxuries: he could have both in India, too. When he had wanted to go to Johns Hopkins for medical training, his parents had loved him enough to let him go. They loved him the same intense, unexamined way he loved his own boy. He had let them down. Perhaps he hadn't really let them down in that he had done well at medical school, and had a job in the State setup in Queens, and played the money market aggressively with a bit of inside information from Suresh Khanna who had been a year ahead of him in Delhi's Modern School and was now with Merrill Lynch, but he hadn't reciprocated their devotion.

It was in this mood of regret filtered through longing that Manny had driven in Manhattan and parked his Porsche on a side-street outside the Sari Palace which was a block up from the New Taj Mahal, where behind the counter he had spied the girl of his dreams.

The girl – the woman, Manny corrected himself instantly, for Camille didn't tolerate what she called 'masculists' – moved out from behind the counter to show a customer where in the crowded store the ten-pound bags of Basmati rice were stacked. She wore a 'Police' T-shirt and navy cords. The cords voluted up her small, rounded thighs and creased around her crotch in a delicate burst, like a Japanese fan. He would have dressed her in a silk sari of peacock blue. He wanted to wrap her narrow wrists in bracelets of 24-carat gold. He wanted to decorate her bosom and throat with necklaces of pearls, rubies, emeralds. She was as lovely and as removed from him as a goddess. He breathed warm, worshipful stains on the dingy store window.

She stooped to pick up a sack of rice by its rough jute handles while the customer flitted across the floor to a bin of eggplants.

3 **Johns Hopkins** University in Baltimore, Maryland, esp. renowned for its medical faculty – 7 **setup** *here:* government-financed organization – 8 **to play the money-market** to speculate on the stock exchange – 10 **Modern School** highly-regarded New Delhi secondary school, founded 1920 – 11 **Merrill Lynch** US investment company – 11 **to reciprocate** to return a favour – 12 **longing** strong desire or hope – 18 **masculist** invented word:*op pod* 'feminist' – 21 **Police** British rock band of the 1970s-80s, with lead singer Sting – 21 **navy cords** dark blue corduroy trousers (*blaue Cordhose*) – 21 **to volute** to make a circular movement, to curve – 22 **to crease** to be crushed into lines – 22 **crotch** part of body between the legs – 23 **fan** hand-held object used to move the air for coolness – 24 **peacock blue** turquoise, colour of the tail feathers of the bird (*Pfau*) – 28 **worshipful** *here:* as if praying – 28 **dingy** ['dɪndʒɪ] dirty – 29 **to stoop** to bend down – 30 **to flit** to move lightly and quickly – 30 **eggplant** aubergine

He discerned a touch of indolence in the way she paused before slipping her snake-slim fingers through the sack's hemp loops. She paused again. She tested the strength of the loops. She bent her knees, ready to heave the brutish sack of rice. He found himself running into the store. He couldn't let her do it. He couldn't let a goddess do menial chores, then ride home on a subway with a backache.

'Oh, thank you,' she said. She flashed him an indolent glance from under heavily shadowed eyelids, without seeming to turn away from the customer who had expected her to lift the ten-pound sack.

Where are the fresh eggplants? These are all dried out.'

Manny Patel watched the customer flick the pleats of her Japanese georgette sari irritably over the sturdy tops of her winter boots.

'These things look as if they've been here all week!' the woman continued to complain.

Manny couldn't bear her beauty. Perfect crimson nails raked the top layer of eggplants. 'They came in just two days ago.'

If there had been room for a third pair of hands, he would have come up with plump, seedless, perfect eggplants.

'Ring up the rice, dal and spices,' the customer instructed. 'I'll get my vegetables next door.'

'I'll take four eggplants,' Manny Patel said defiantly. 'And two pounds of *bhindi*.' He sorted through wilted piles of okra which Camille wouldn't know how to cook.

'I'll be with you in a minute, sir,' the goddess answered.

When she looked up again, he asked her out for dinner. She only said, 'You really don't have to buy anything, you know.'

She suggested they meet outside the Sari Palace at six thirty. Her readiness overwhelmed him. Dr Patel had been out of the business of dating for almost thirteen years. At conferences, on

1 **to discern** to notice – 1 **indolence** ['ɪndələns] laziness – 2 **hemp** rope made from fibres of the cannabis plant (*Hanf*) – 4 **brutish** like a rough animal – 6 **menial chore** unskilled job – 13 **to flick** to hit lightly with the fingers – 13 **pleats** folds – 14 **georgette** thin silk or cotton crepe cloth – 14 **irritably** showing signs of being easily annoyed – 14 **sturdy** solid and strong – 18 **crimson** deep red – 18 **to rake** to scrape, as if with the garden tool (*Rechen*) – 21 **plump** fat – 22 **dal** (*Hindi*) kind of lentils (*Linsen*) – 22 **spice** sth which adds flavour to food – 25 **bhindi** (*Hindi*) a vegetable known as okra or lady's fingers – 25 **to wilt** to wither, become old and dry – 31 **to overwhelm** to be strongly emotionally affected – 32 **dating** (*AE*) going out with a person because of sexual interest

trips and on the occasional night in the city when an older self possessed him, he would hire women for the evening, much as he had done in India. They were never precisely the answer, not even to his desire.

Camille had taken charge as soon as she had spotted him in the hospital cafeteria; she had done the pursuing. While he did occasionally flirt with a Filipino nutritionist at the hospital where he now worked, he assumed he did not possess the dexterity to perform the two-step dance of assertiveness and humility required of serious adultery. He left the store flattered but wary. A goddess had found him attractive, but he didn't know her name. He didn't know what kind of family fury she might unleash on him. Still, for the first time in years he felt a kind of agitated discovery, as though if he let up for a minute, his reconstituted, instant American life would not let him back.

His other self, the sober, greedy, scholarly Dr Patel, knew that life didn't change that easily. He had seen enough Horowitzes to know that no matter how astute his own methods might be and no matter how miraculous the discoveries of psychopharmacologists, fate could not be derailed. How did it come about that Mr Horowitz, the son of a successful slacks manufacturer, a good student at the Bronx High School of Science, had ended up obese, disturbed and assaultive, while he, the son of a Gujarati farmer turned entrepreneur, an indifferent student at Modern School and then at St. Stephen's in Delhi, was ambitious and acquisitive? All his learning and experience could not answer the simplest questions. He had about an hour and twenty minutes to kill before perfection was to revisit him, this time (he guessed) in full glory.

5 **to take charge** to be actively responsible – 7 **nutritionist** expert in food requirements and and diet – 9 **dexterity** ability to make complicated movements, agility – 9 **assertiveness** confidence, ability to express one's wishes – 10 **humility** state pof being humble – 10 **adultery** extramarital sex – 10 **flattered** feeling pleased at sb's high opinion of os – 11 **wary** careful – 12 **fury** great anger – 13 **to unleash** to let loose – 14 **agitated** disturbed – 14 **to let up** to stop or lessen one's efforts – 15 **reconstituted** *here:* created anew – 16 **sober** serious – 18 **astute** wise, clever – 19 **miraculous** wonderful, like a miracle – 20 **fate** what must happen (*Schicksal*) – 20 **to derail** to knock (a train) off the tracks (*here fig*) – 21 **slacks** casual trousers – 22 **Bronx** borough of New York city – 23 **obese** fat, overweight – 23 **assaultive** physically aggressive – 24 **Gujarati** native of Gujarat, a state in north-west India – 24 **entrepreneur** (*French*) business person – 24 **indifferent** *here:* middling, not very good – 26 **ambitious** wanting to achieve great things – 26 **acquisitive** trying to get things

Dr Patel wandered through 'Little India' – the busy, colourful blocks of Indian shops and restaurants off Lexington in the upper twenties. Men lugged heavy crates out of doubleparked pickup trucks, swearing in Punjabi and Hindi. Women with tired, frightened eyes stepped into restaurants, careful not to drop their shopping-sacks from Bloomingdale's and Macy's. The Manhattan air here was fragrant with spices. He followed an attractive mother with two preschoolers into Chandni Chowk, a tea and snacks-stall, to call Camille about the emergency that had come up. Thank god for Mr Horowitz's recidivism. Camille was familiar with the more outrageous doings of Mr Horowitz.

'Why does that man always act up when I have plans?' Camille demanded. '*Amarcord* is at the rep tonight only.'

But Camille seemed in as agreeable a mood as his goddess. She thought she might ask Susan Kwan, the wife of an orthodontist who lived four houses up the block and who had a son by a former marriage also at Andover. Her credulousness depressed Manny. A woman who had lived with a man for almost thirteen years should be able to catch his little lies.

'Mr Horowitz is a dangerous person,' he continued. He could have hung up, but he didn't. He didn't want permission; he wanted sympathy. 'He rushed into my office. He tried to kill me.'

'Maybe psychiatrists at state institutions ought to carry firearms. Have you thought of that, Manny?' she laughed.

Manny Patel flushed. Camille didn't understand how the job was draining him. Mr Horowitz had, for a fact, flopped like a walrus on Dr Patel's desk, demanding a press conference so that the world would know that his civil liberties were being

2 **Lexington** (in Manhattan, New York) avenue between Third Ave. and Park Ave. – 3 **twenties** *here:* the Manhatten streets numbered from 20th to 29th – 3 **to lug** to carry (sth heavy) – 3 **crate** large box – 4 **pickup truck** (*AE*) small lorry with open back – 4 **to swear** *here;* to use bad language, to curse – 4 **Punjabi** language of Punjab, state in central India (related to Hindi, the national language) – 6 **Bloomingdale's, Macy's** Manhattan department stores – 7 **fragrant** ['freɪgrənt] pleasant smelling – 8 **Chandni Chowk** main street of Old Delhi, a busy shopping bazaar; *here:* a shop called after it – 10 **recidivism** tendency to relapse, i.e. become ill again – 11 **outrageous** strange and shocking – 13 **Amarcord** Italian film (1973) directed by Frederico Fellini – 13 **rep** short for 'repertory', which describes a (stage or film) theatre with frequently changing programme – 15 **orthodontist** dentist specialized in straightening teeth – 17 **credulousness** willingness to believe; *opp* of scepticism – 25 **firearms** guns – 26 **to flush** to go red in the face – 27 **to drain** to make sb lose energy, become tired – 27 **to flop** to fall loosely

infringed. The moneyless schizos of New York state, Mr Horowitz had screamed, were being held hostage by a bunch of foreign doctors who couldn't speak English. If it hadn't been for the two six-foot orderlies (Dr Patel felt an awakening of respect for big blacks), Mr Horowitz would probably have grabbed him by the throat.

'I could have died today,' he repeated. The realization dazed him. The man tried to strangle me.'

He hung up and ordered a cup of masala tea. The sweet, sticky brew calmed him, and the perfumed steam cleared his sinuses. Another man in his position would probably have ordered a double Scotch. In crises, he seemed to regress, to reach automatically for the miracle cures of his Delhi youth, though normally he had no patience with nostalgia. When he had married, he burned his India Society membership card. He was professionally cordial, nothing more, with Indian doctors at the hospital. But he knew he would forever shuttle between the old world and the new. He couldn't pretend he had been reborn when he became an American citizen in a Manhattan courthouse. Rebirth was the privilege of the dead, and of gods and goddesses, and they could leap into your life in myriad, mysterious ways, as a shopgirl, for instance, or as a withered eggplant, just to test you.

At three minutes after six, Dr Patel positioned himself inside his Porsche and watched the front doors of the Sari Palace for his date's arrival. He didn't want to give the appearance of having waited nervously. There was a slight tremor in both his hands. He was suffering a small attack of anxiety. At thirty-three minutes after six, she appeared in the doorway of the sari-store. She came out of the Sari Palace, not up the street from the New Taj Mahal as he had expected. He slammed shut and locked his car door. Did it mean that she too had come to the rendezvous too early and had spied on him, crouched, anxious, strapped in the bucket seat of his Porsche? When he caught up with her

1 **to infringe** to violate, fail to respect – 1 **schizos** = schizophrenics (*usu derog*) – 2 **to hold hostage** to keep sb by force in order to make some demand – 4 **orderly** *here:* male hospital attendant – 8 **to strangle** to kill by squeezing sb's neck – 9 **masala** (*Hindi*) spiced – 12 **crises** ['kraɪsi:z] *pl* of 'crisis' – 12 **to regress** to fall back to an earlier stage of development – 16 **cordial** friendly – 17 **to shuttle** to constantly move between two points (*here fig*) – 21 **myriad** many and varied – 26 **date** *here:* person one is dating – 27 **tremor** small shake – 28 **anxiety** [□ŋg'zaɪətɪ] nervousness – 31 **to slam** to close with a bang – 33 **crouched** bent down – 34 **bucket** *here:* curved to fit around the body

by the store window, she was the most beautiful woman he had ever talked to.

Her name was Padma. She told him that as he fought for a cab to take them uptown. He didn't ask for, and she didn't reveal, her last name. Both were aware of the illicit nature of their meeting. An Indian man his age had to be married, though he wore no wedding ring. An immigrant girl from a decent Hindu family – it didn't matter how long she had lived in America and what rock groups she was crazy about – would not have said yes to dinner with a man she didn't know. It was this inarticulate unsanctionedness of the dinner date that made him feel reckless, a hedonist, a man who might trample tired ladies carrying shopping-bags in order to steal a taxi crawling uptown. He wanted to take Padma to an Indian restaurant so that he would feel he knew what he was ordering and could bully the maitre d' a bit, but not to an Indian restaurant in her neighbourhood. He wanted a nice Indian restaurant, an upscale one, with tablecloths, sitar music and air ducts sprayed with the essence of rose-petals. He chose a new one, Shajahan, on Park Avenue.

'It's nice. I was going to recommend it,' she said.

Padma. Lotus. The goddess had come to him as a flower. He wanted to lunge for her hands as soon as they had been seated at a corner booth, but he knew better than to frighten her off. He was mortal, he was humble.

The *maitre d'* himself took Dr Patel's order. And with the *hors d' oeuvres* of *samosas* and *poppadoms* he sent a bottle of Entre Deux Mers on the house. Dr Patel had dined at the Shajahan four or five times already, and each time had brought in a group of six or eight. He had been a little afraid that the *maitre d'* might disapprove of his bringing a youngish woman, an Indian and

5 **to reveal** to make known – 5 **illicit** not allowed, against social rules – 8 **decent** respectable – 11 **inarticulate unsanctionedness** sense that sth is forbidden without being able to express it – 12 **reckless** careless, with no regard for safety – 12 **hedonist** sb who is only interested in pleasure – 16 **to bully** to terrorize – 16 **maitre d'(hotel)** (*French*) head waiter – 17 **upscale** high class – 18 **sitar** stringed instrument used a lot in Indian classical music – 18 **duct** vent, opening for air to pass through – 24 **booth** partially closed off table – 25 **mortal** capable of dying, human – 26 **hors d'oeuvres** (*French*) starters – 27 **samosa** Indian snack (meat and/or vegetables wrapped in pastry) – 27 **poppadom** crispy Indian bread – 27 **Entre Deux Mers** (*French*) dry white wine from an area east of Bordeaux between two sea inlets – 28 **on the house** free

quite obviously not his wife, but the bottle of wine reassured him that the management was not judgemental.

He broke off a sliver of *poppadom* and held it to her lips. She snatched it with an exaggerated flurry of lips and teeth: 'Feeding the performing seal, are you?' She was coy. And amused.

'I didn't mean it that way,' he murmured. Her lips, he noticed, had left a glistening crescent of lipstick on a fingertip. He wiped the finger with his napkin surreptitiously under the table.

She didn't help herself to the samosas, and he didn't dare lift a forkful to her mouth. Perhaps she didn't care for samosas. Perhaps she wasn't much of an eater. He himself was timid and clumsy, half afraid that if he tried anything playful he might drip mint chutney on her tiger-print -chiffon sari.

'Do you mind if I smoke?'

He busied himself with food while she took out a packet of Sobrani and a book of matches. Camille had given up smoking four years before, and now handwritten instructions THANK YOU FOR NOT SMOKING IN THIS HOUSE decorated bureautops and coffee tables. He had never got started because of an allergy.

'Well?' she said. It wasn't quite a question, and it wasn't quite a demand. 'Aren't you going to light it?' And she offered Manny Patel an exquisite profile, cheeks sucked tight and lips squeezed around the filter tip.

The most banal gesture of a goddess can destroy a decent-living mortal. He lit her cigarette, then blew the match out with a gust of unreasonable hope.

The *maitre d'* hung around Manny's table almost to the point of neglecting other early diners. He had sad eyes and a bushy moustache. He wore a dark suit, a silvery wide tie kept in place with an elephant-headed god stick-pin, and on his feet which were remarkably large for a short, slight man, scuffed and pointed black shoes.

2 **not judgemental** neutral, not judging or critical of sb's behaviour – 3 **sliver** small thin piece – 4 **to snatch** to grab – 4 **flurry** rushed movements – 5 **seal** sea animal (*Seehund*) often in circuses for entertainment – 5 **coy** making a show of shyness – 7 **crescent** half-moon shape – 8 **surreptitiously** secretly, being careful not to be seen – 12 **clumsy** awkward – 13 **chutney** jam-like food addition, made with vegetables, sugar, and vinegar – 13 **chiffon** [ˈʃɪfɒn] a very loosely-woven silk or cotton – 16 **Sobrani** brand of Russian cigarettes – 19 **bureautop** desktop – 27 **gust** sudden blow of wind or air – 29 **to neglect** to fail to pay attention to – 31 **elephant-headed god** probably the Hindu god Ganesha – 32 **scuffed** slightly damaged by rubbing

'I wouldn't recommend the pork vindaloo tonight.' The man's voice was confidential, low. 'We have a substitute cook. But the fish Bengal curry is very good. The lady, I think, is Bengali, no?'

She did not seem surprised. 'How very observant of you, sir,' she smiled.

It was flattering to have the *maitre d'* linger and advise. Manny Patel ended up ordering one each of the curries listed under beef, lamb and fowl. He was a guiltlessly meat-eating Gujarati, at least in America. He filled in the rest of the order with two vegetable dishes, one spiced lentil and a vegetable *pilau*. The *raita* was free, as were the two small jars of mango and lemon pickle.

When the food started coming, Padma reluctantly stubbed out her Sobrani. The *maitre d'* served them himself, making clucking noises with his tongue against uneven, oversize teeth, and Dr Patel felt obliged to make loud appreciative moans.

'Is everything fine, doctor sahib?' Fish is first class, no? It is not on the regular menu.'

He stayed and made small talk about Americans. He dispatched waiters to other tables, directing them with claps of pinkish palms from the edge of Manny's booth. Padma made an initial show of picking at her vegetable *pilau*. Then she gave up and took out another slim black Sobrani from a tin packet and held her face, uplifted and radiant, close to Manny's so he could light it again for her.

The *maitre d'* said, 'I'm having a small problem, doctor sahib. Actually the problem is my wife's. She has been in America three years and she is very lonely still. I'm saying to her, you have nice apartment in Rego Park, you have nice furnitures and fridge and stove, I'm driving you here and there in a blue Buick, you're having home-style Indian food, what then is wrong? But I am knowing and you are knowing, doctor sahib, that no Indian lady

1 **vindaloo** a hot, spicy dish – 2 **confidential** *here:* as if passing on a secret – 3 **Bengali** [beŋ'gɔ:lɪ] native of Bengal, a state in north-east India – 6 **to linger** ['lɪŋgə] to wait around – 8 **fowl** birds used as food (e.g. chicken) – 10 **pilau** rice dish with meat or vegetable pieces – 11 **raita** flavoured yoghurt used to make spicy dishes milder – 12 **pickle** vegetable preserved in vinegar – 13 **reluctantly** unwillingly – 13 **to stub out** to quench (a cigarette) by pressing against sth – 16 **appreciative moan** sound that usually expresses pain, but here, enjoyment – 17 **sahib** (*Hindi*) term of respect for a man – 20 **to dispatch** to send – 21 **palm** inner surface of the hand – 22 **initial** at the beginning – 24 **radiant** ['reɪdɪənt] shining with happiness or pleasure – 30 **Buick** ['bjʊɪk] American make of car

is happy without having children to bring up. That is why, in my desperation, I brought over my sister's child last June. We want to adopt him, he is very bright and talented and already he is loving this country. But the US government is telling me no. The boy came on a visitor's visa, and now the government is giving me big trouble. They are calling me bad names. Jealous peoples are telling them bad stories. They are saying I'm in the business of moving illegal aliens, can you believe? In the meantime, my wife is crying all day and pulling out her hair. Doctor sahib, you can write that she needs to have the boy here for her peace of mind and mental stability, no? On official stationery of your hospital, doctor sahib?'

'My hands are tied,' Manny Patel said. 'The US government wouldn't listen to me.'

Padma said nothing. Manny ignored the *maitre d'*. A reality was dawning on Manny Patel. It was too beautiful, too exciting to contemplate. He didn't want this night to fall under the pressure of other immigrants' woes.

'But you will write a letter about my wife's mental problems, doctor sahib?' The *maitre d'* had summoned up tears. A man in a dark suit weeping in an upscale ethnic restaurant. Manny felt slightly disgraced, he wished the man would go away. 'Official stationery is very necessary to impress the immigration people.'

'Please leave us alone,' snapped Manny Patel. 'If you persist I will never come back.'

The old assurance, the authority of a millionaire in his native culture, was returning. He was sure of himself.

'What do you want to do after dinner?' Padma asked when the *maitre d'* scurried away from their booth. Manny could sense him, wounded and scowling, from behind the kitchen door.

'What would you like to do?' He thought of his wife and Mrs Kwan at the Fellini movie. They would probably have a drink at a bar before coming home. Susan Kwan had delightful legs. He had trouble understanding her husband, but Manny Patel had spent enjoyable hours at the Kwans', watching Mrs Kwan's legs.

8 **alien** ['eɪlɪən] *here:* foreigner – 11 **stationery** writing paper – 16 **to dawn on** to begin to become clear – 18 **woe** trouble, sth that causes worry – 20 **to summon** to call up – 22 **to disgrace** to embarrass – 25 **to persist** to keep on doing sth – 30 **to scurry** to to move quickly with small steps – 31 **to scowl** to frown angrily

Padma's legs remained a mystery; he had seen her only in pants or a sari.

'If you are thinking of fucking me,' she said very suddenly, 'I should warn you that I never have an orgasm. You won't have to worry about pleasing me.'

Yes, he thought, it is so, just as he had suspected. It was a night in which he could do no wrong. He waved his visa card at the surly *maitre d'* and paid the bill. After that Padma let him take her elbow and guide her to the expensive hotel above the restaurant.

An oriental man at the desk asked him, 'Cash or credit card, sir?' He paid for a double occupancy room with cash and signed himself in as Dr Mohan Vakil & wife, 18 Ridgewood Drive, Columbus, Ohio.

He had laid claim to America.

In a dark seventh-floor room off a back corridor, the goddess bared her flesh to a dazed, daunted mortal. She was small. She was perfect. She had saucy breasts, fluted thighs and tiny, taut big toes.

'Hey, you can suck but don't bite, okay?' Padma may have been slow to come, but he was not. He fell on her with a devotee's frenzy.

'Does it bother you?' she asked later, smoking the second Sobrani. She was on her side. Her tummy had a hint of convex opulence. 'About my not getting off?'

He couldn't answer. It was a small price to pay, and anyway he wasn't paying it. Nothing could diminish the thrill he felt in taking a chance. It wasn't the hotel and this bed; it was having stepped inside the New Taj Mahal and asking her out.

He should probably call home, in case Camille hadn't stopped off for a drink. He should probably get dressed, offer her something generous – as discreetly as possible, for this one had class, real class – then drive himself home. The Indian food, an Indian woman in bed, made him nostalgic. He wished he were in his kitchen, and that his parents were visiting him and

3 **to fuck** (*vulg*) to have sex with – 8 **surly** ill-humoured – 15 **to lay claim to** to to establish ownership of – 17 **dazed** bewildered, slightly shocked – 17 **daunted** intimidated, made nervous – 18 **saucy** (*inf*) cheeky (*here fig*) – 21 **to come** *here:* to have an orgasm – 21 **devotee** [ˌdevəʊ'ti:] religious follower – 22 **frenzy** wild excitement – 24 **convex** wih an outward curve – 25 **opulence** fullness – 25 **to get off** *here:* to have an orgasm

that his mother was making him a mug of hot Horlick's and that his son was not so far removed from him in a boarding school.

He wished he had married an Indian woman. One that his father had selected. He wished he had any life but the one he had chosen.

As Dr Patel sat on the edge of the double bed and slid his feet through the legs of his trousers, someone rapped softly on the hotel door, then without waiting for an answer unlocked it with a passkey.

Padma pulled the sheet up to her chin, but did not seem to have been startled.

'She's underage, of course,' the *maitre d'* said. 'She is my sister's youngest daughter. I accuse you of rape, doctor sahib. You are of course ruined in this country. You have everything and think you must have more. You are highly immoral.'

He sat on the one chair that wasn't littered with urgently cast-off clothes, and lit a cigarette. It was rapidly becoming stuffy in the room, and Manny's eyes were running. The man's eyes were malevolent, but the rest of his face remained practised and relaxed. An uncle should have been angrier, Dr Patel thought automatically. He himself should have seen it coming. He had mistaken her independence as a bold sign of honest assimilation. But it was his son who was the traveller over shifting sands, not her.

There was no point in hurrying. Meticulously he put on his trousers, double-checked the zipper, buttoned his shirt, knotted his tie and slipped on his Gucci shoes. *The lady is Bengali, no?* Yes, they knew one another, perhaps even as uncle and niece. Or pimp and hooker. The air here was polluted with criminality. He wondered if his slacks had been made by immigrant women in Mr Horowitz's father's sweat-shop.

'She's got to be at least twenty-three, twenty-four,' Dr Patel said. He stared at her, deliberately insolent. Through the sheets

1 **Horlick's** a malted milk drink supposed to promote sleep; made in UK and India – 12 **underage** too young (legally) – 13 **rape** crime of forced sex – 16 **urgently cast off** thrown off hurriedly, as if in an emergency – 17 **stuffy** airless, hard to breathe – 18 **running** *here:* wet, dripping with water – 19 **malevolent** [mə'levələnt] evil, wishing to do harm – 23 **assimilation** adaptation to the culture of the country – 24 **shifting** moving, instable – 25 **meticulously** with great care and attention to detail – 29 **pimp** (*inf*) man who lives off a prostitute's earnings (*Zuhälter*) – 29 **hooker** (*inf*) prostitute – 31 **sweat-shop** (*inf*) factory or workshop where workers are exploited for low wages – 33 **insolent** showing no respect

he could make out the upward thrust of her taut big toes. He had kissed those toes only half-an-hour before. He must have been mad.

'I'm telling you she is a minor. I'm intending to make a citizen's arrest. I have her passport in my pocket.'

It took an hour of bickering and threats to settle. He made out a check for seven hundred dollars. He would write a letter on hospital stationery. The uncle made assurances that there were no hidden tapes. Padma went into the bathroom to wash up and dress.

'Why?' Manny shouted, but he knew Padma couldn't hear him over the noise of the gushing faucet.

After the team left him, Manny Patel took off his clothes and went into the bathroom so recently used by the best-looking woman he had ever talked to (or slept with, he could now add). Her perfume, he thought of it as essence of lotus, made him choke.

He pulled himself up, using the edge of the bathtub as a step ladder, until his feet were on the wide edges of the old-fashioned sink. Then, squatting like a villager, squatting the way he had done in his father's home, he defecated into the sink, and with handfuls of his own shit – it felt hot, light, porous, an artist's medium – he wrote WHORE on the mirror and floor.

He spent the night in the hotel room. Just before dawn he took a cab to the parking lot of the Sari Palace. Miraculously, no vandals had touched his Porsche. Feeling lucky, spared somehow in spite of his brush with the deities, he drove home.

Camille had left the porch light on and it glowed pale in the brightening light of the morning. In a few hours Mr Horowitz would start to respond to the increased dosage of Haldol and be let out of the seclusion chamber. At the end of the term, Shawn Patel would come home from Andover and spend all day in the house with earphones tuned to a happier world. And in August, he would take his wife on a cruise through the Caribbean and make up for this night with a second honeymoon.

1 **thrust** push – 1 **taut** held tightly – 4 **minor** *here:* sb under a certain legal age – 6 **to bicker** to quarrel – 9 **tapes** *here:* videotape recordings – 12 **to gush** to flow strongly – 12 **faucet** ['fɔ:sɪt] (*AE*) tap – 20 **to squat** [skwɒt] to bend so as to nearly sit on a surface – 21 **to defecate** (*form*) to empty one's bowels – 23 **whore** (*inf*) prostitute – 27 **brush** *here:* short but unpleasant contact – 27 **deity** ['di:ɪtɪ] god – 30 **to respond** *here:* to react – 34 **cruise** pleasure trip on a ship – 35 **to make up for** to compensate for – 35 **honeymoon** holiday taken by a newly-married couple

Additional Materials

1. English in India: Still All the Raj

The assault began, really, as soon as I set foot in Bombay a few months before the golden jubilee of Indian independence. "If Aggrieved," advised the sign in the airport arrival hall, "Please Consult Asstt. Commissioner Customs." At the counter where I went to change my money, a notice told me, "PLEASE ENSURE THAT YOUR DRAWERS ARE LOCKED PROPERLY," and after I'd done so, looking down demurely, I stepped into a wheezing old knock-off of a Morris Oxford to lurch through streets that said "Free Left Turn" on one side and "Passenger Alighting Point" on the other. The crazy Indian dialectic was in full swing all around, buses demanding "SILENCE PLEASE" on their exteriors, a few truck mudguards responding, "HORN O.K. PLEASE," and my own little car making its own small contribution to democracy with a sticker that read: "Blow Your Horn / Pay a Fine."

India is the most talkative country in the world, it often seems, and it comes at you in almost 200 languages, 1,652 dialects and a million signs and slogans screaming out of every store and taxicab. Many of them are just familiar enough to be quite strange. We passed Textoriums as we drove into town, and a Toilet Complex, Stomach Trimmer palaces and Police Beat Boxes. We passed the Clip Joint Beauty Clinic and Nota Bene Cleaners of Distinction. A sign outside one apartment block offered: "No Parking for Out Siders. If Found Guilty, All Tyres Will Be Deflated With Extreme Prejudice." An ad for a lecture informed me that

the Raj British rule in India before 1947; *here:* a pun on 'all the rage', i.e. in fashion – 1 **assault** attack – 3 **to aggrieve** (*form*) to cause distress or upset – 4 **Asstt.** = Assistant – 6 **drawers** 1. openable, sliding compartments in a desk; 2. underpants – 7 **demurely** as if shy or modest – 7 **wheezing** making unhealthy sounds (*usu* of breathing) – 8 **knock-off** copy, imitation – 8 **Morris Oxford** old-fashioned British make of car (the Indian 'Ambassador' is similar) – 8 **to lurch** to move suddenly and unsteadily – 9 **to alight** (*form*) to step out of, or down from (a vehicle) – 12 **mudguard** part of vehicle over a wheel – 20 **beat** *here (probably):* patrol – 21 **clip joint** *usu* disreputable pub or restaurant where customers are overcharged – 23 **to deflate** to let the air out of – 24 **with extreme prejudice** (*legal phrase*) negatively affecting one's rights

"Yogic laughter is multidimensional." I could only imagine that like most of the city's notices, it had been fashioned by some proud graduate of the course I saw advertised in the local newspaper: "We make you big boss in English conversation. Hypnotize people by your highly impressive talks. Exclusive courses for exporters, business tycoons."

Malcolm Muggeridge famously remarked that the last true Englishman would be an Indian, and it's easy to believe that when you hear the "jolly goods" and "out of station chappies" ricocheting around the Willingdon Club in Bombay, or any of the other old canteens and cantonments and Civil List houses that fill the country's dusty enclaves. Much of the fascination of Indian English lies in the fact that it is as flavorful a monument to the Raj as the white-flannel cricketers along the Oval, the "Whispering Pines" cottages around the hills and the mossy, overgrown gravestones commemorating forgotten personages like Sarah Chandy and the Bombay Color Sergeants.

But a deeper fascination is that modern India has so thoroughly made the language imposed on it its own, so vigorously adding condiments that it isn't quite English and isn't quite not. The history of Indlish or Englian, or whatever you want to call this hyperactive offspring of a marriage of inconvenience, begins with the merchants and adventurers of the East India Company, who first came over in the mid-17th century, and were soon taking back cashmeres and juggernauts and other semi-demi-pukka terms stolen from the Indian Empire. But it culminated most vividly in the soldiers and teachers and high-minded

1 **yogic** of yoga – 3 **graduate** sb who has successfully completed an educational course – 6 **tycoon** (*usu derog*) very powerful and rich businessman – 7 **Malcolm Muggeridge** (1903-1990) English writer and social commentator – 9 **chappie** diminuative of 'chap' = fellow; an example of upper-class military slang – 10 **to ricochet** (*from French*) ['rɪkəʃeɪ] *here:* to echo – 11 **canteen** *here:* military recreation area – 11 **cantonment** military residential area – 11 **Civil List** financed by the British government – 14 **the Oval** cricket grounds in London – 17 **colo(u)r sergeant** ['sɑːdʒənt] officer carrying the colours of a regiment – 20 **condiment** spice – 22 **offspring of ...** child of ... (the following phrase reverses the more usual 'marriage of convenience') – 23 **merchant** trader – 25 **cashmere** very fine wool from a goat found in the Himalayas, esp. Kashmir – 25 **juggernaut** (*from Hindi*) originally a Hindu god carried as an idol on a huge chariot; now, a very large lorry for transporting goods throughout Europe – 26 **pukka** (*from Hindi*) genuine, properly constructed

civil servants of later centuries, who made it their business to domesticate the East, and often got thoroughly domesticated themselves. We all know that Victoria sent railroads and bewigged solicitors and Thomas Babington Macaulay to India; what we're liable to forget is that by the middle of the 19th century, according to one account, India had sent 26,000 words back into English, many of them as familiar as your pajamas or veranda. [...]

Nowadays, as Salman Rushdie notes, imperialism is reversed not only on the page, and any Englishman worth his salt – any tycoon or pundit or thug, in fact – knows all about gurus and mantras and yoga. "They gave us the language," as a character says in Hanif Kureishi's novel *The Black Album*, "but it is only we who know how to use it." Those who marvel at the rutputty masala mixes in Rushdie's novels are apt to exaggerate the magic and underestimate the realism. A walk down any Bombay street is not unlike a journey through any chapter of *Midnight's Children*. [...]

It is as if words in the subcontinent were still assumed to have a magic they've lost at home, as if calling a place "Reliable" or "Honesty" were the first step toward making it so. Not that Indian courtesy is always innocent. "Any Exchange Fault or Communications Error," a sign in a public phone office advised me, "Is on Customer's Account. Thanks." Some of the terms you see in India have curious meanings (the cafes advertising "fingers," I learned, were only selling "finger chips," or french fries), and some of them just look as if they do. ("Video Shooting We Undertake," a tiny photo shop informed me.) Some meticulously preserve now fading customs, and some confer a gay Edwardian tilt on even the most everyday transactions. ("I'm sorry," I was told when I called up the editor of a movie magazine, "Miss

1 **civil servant** government employee – 4 **bewigged solicitors** lawyers wearing wigs – 4 **Thomas Babington Macauley** (1800-59) British essayist and historian – 8 **Salman Rushdie** see p. 40 – 10 **pundit** (*from Hindi*) learned person, expert on a topic – 10 **thug** (*from Hindi*) rough criminal, hooligan – 12 **Hanif Kureishi** (b. 1954) Indian-English writer – 13 **to marvel** to wonder, be impressed by – 13 **rutputty masala** ... roughly, 'shabby and spicy'; see p. 51 – 14 **apt to** likely to – 20 **reliable** [rɪˈlaɪəbl] trustworthy, can be relied on – 21 **courtesy** [ˈkɜːtɪsɪ] good manners, politeness – 28 **to undertake** 1. to take on a job; 2. to arrange burials – 27 **meticulously** with great care for detail – 28 **to confer** [kənˈfɜː] to give, provide – 28 **gay Edwardian tilt** light-hearted style typical of the reign of Edward VII (1901-10)

Sonaya is not in her cabin just now," which made me imagine her, perhaps not incorrectly, on a cruise ship.) At Elphinstone College, in the redbrick Victorian heart of the University of Bombay, I was greeted by an "Institute of Distance Education" just down the corridor from a "Backward Class Cell." And in the city's most famous Hindu temple a sign advised, "Devotees are warned that to sit on the rocks much deep in the sea water away from the sea shore is not only encroachment on government property but is also dangerous to their lives, including valuable ornaments."

Whether or not my life was a valuable ornament, I came away feeling that Indian English is not just a savory stepmother tongue to hundreds of millions of Indians (more Indians, after all, speak English than Englishmen do), and not just an invaluable memento of a centuries-long mishmash, but also a grand and distinctive product of a culture as verbally supple and full of energy as any I know. Six years ago, India at last opened its borders wide to foreign companies, and when last I was in Bombay, "cyberprofessional" and "brand name equity" were the terms of the moment, bandied about by the young in their MTV-furnished pubs, as they spoke with studied casualness of "air-dashing." In the newspapers, editorials that still drew, with surprising frequency, upon the example and wisdom of Bertram Wooster sat next to ads that promised a "Mega Exhibition Showcase of Ideal Lifestyle."

Yet this stubbornly anachronistic tongue, out of date even when it was first imported, suggests that there'll always be an England, if only because there'll always be an India. As I prepared to air-dash away – being asked my "good name" one last time, in Delhi's airport [...] – I wondered how far I was really going. "Blighty," after all, is the Hindi word for "foreign."

Article by Pico Iyer, from *The New York Times*, August 10, 1997 (abridged).

6 **devotee** follower of a religion – 8 **encroachment** intrusion, trespass – 11 **savory** tasty, spicy – 11 **stepmother tongue** *here:* near-native language – 15 **supple** flexible – 18 **equity** ['ekwɪtɪ] *here:* market value – 18 **to bandy about** to throw around, use freely – 19 **MTV-furnished** decorated in the style of this satellite TV channel (devoted to pop music) – 22 **Bertram Wooster** (better known as 'Bertie Wooster') upper-class character in the comic novels of P.G. Wodehouse (1881-1875) – 24 **stubbornly anachronistic** determined to belong to a different time – 25 **there'll always be ...** line from (and title of) a popular patriotic song (1940) by Charles Hughes – 28 **Blighty** (*BE slang, dated*) England, home

2. Relative Values: Anita Desai and her Daughter Kiran

Though Anita Desai was shortlisted for the Booker Prize several times (in 1980, 1984, and 1999) she never won it outright. Her daughter Kiran, however, was awarded the prestigious prize for her novel The Inheritance of Loss *in 2006. In separate interviews for a British newspaper feature, mother and daughter reflect on their relationship and their experiences of writing and emigration.*

Anita: My children always said they would never be writers. They'd tell me I led the most boring life of anyone they had ever seen. Kiran was a great reader – a book a day. But she didn't write. She didn't show any interest in it until college. When she showed me her first stories, I knew I should see to it that she had the time, space and encouragement to write – it came to her so easily.

I wanted to give her the support that I lacked as a young writer. Neighbours in New Delhi would say: "I hear you write. What a nice hobby!" It was seen as an eccentricity. I had to send manuscripts to England to be published, and the literary world seemed very far away. It was a frustration, and I felt something was lacking from my life – I had home and family, but nothing beyond that.

I never wrote when the children were around. I trained myself to write according to the academic timetable, starting as soon as they left for school and stopping when they came back. And I put any work in progress away during their vacations. The children hated seeing my manuscripts or published books. They would be upset if they saw my name in the papers in book reviews. I suppose they wanted to keep our relationship private. They thought that if you are a mother, that is all you should be.

1 **shortlisted** among the finalists for a prize – 2 **outright** fully – 4 **inheritance** sth received from a past generation – 5 **feature** article on a special topic – 17 **eccentricity** [ˌeksənˈtrɪsɪtɪ] strange habit –25 **in progress** being worked on at the moment – 25 **vacation** (*AE*) holiday

They had to grow up before they could bear it. It must be a shock to realise a person you thought you knew has another life. And I didn't directly draw on my family life for my books, but there's a lot they could have recognised.

I think it was equally difficult for my husband [Ashvin Desai] – he never objected to my writing, but it is so much easier if you know your mate completely, and I was working on things he knew nothing about. It was never our intention to separate, but I took one step after the other, which made it inevitable.

When Kiran was 15, I was invited to go to the University of Cambridge as a visiting fellow for a year. The other children had already grown up and left home, but I took her along with me. In Cambridge I found, for the first time, a place where freedom and independence of thought were encouraged. I found people who had actually read my books and were encouraging me to write more. So I then accepted an invitation to teach in the US, and took Kiran there with me too. Eventually, I was so used to being independent that it would have been hard to go back to being half of a couple, or part of a family. But the move from India to the West was more difficult for Kiran than for me – much more so than I realised at the time. I felt very guilty when it came spilling out years later, how hard she had found the transition.

Kiran worked in my house a lot during the eight years she spent writing *The Inheritance of Loss*. When she was shortlisted for the Booker prize, I was so frightened for her in case she lost. When it happened to me, I was far away in India, so I had no idea how important it was. By the time I had realised, I had published so much, it somehow mattered less. But I was afraid that not winning might really disappoint Kiran. I tried to tell her that just being shortlisted showed she was one of the top writers. She'd keep telling herself that too. But I made sure I was in India when the prize was given. I couldn't take the tension, and anyway it was Kiran's time and I wanted her to have it to herself. It was wonderful that Kiran won it. She's not my rival, she's my

7 **mate** wife or husband – 9 **inevitable** [ɪn'evɪtəbl] unavoidable – 11 **Cambridge** prestigioius old university north of London – 11 **fellow** *here:* member of the college staff – 22 **transition** change

daughter, so what she does is almost as if I'd done it myself – it's as pleasing for me as for her.

I know Kiran will start another book soon, and I hope she will also start a family. We are very close, because it is a mother-daughter relationship and also a working relationship. But it worries me that her life is so tied up with mine. She doesn't live with me all the time – she has a flat in Brooklyn, and comes and goes from my house near New York. She has an independent nature and loads of friends, so I'm sure she'll find a partner. It is important for her to have someone else in her life – not just her mother!

Kiran: I was aware from an early age that my mother was very unusual, and that feeling has never left me. She was strikingly different from all the other women in the neighbourhood. Most were housewives with businessman husbands who organised parties and did charitable work in their spare time. My mother was never interested in any of that. Not interested in producing the Indian and English versions of dishes and serving them along the two sides of the table, not interested in dressing up in elaborate silk saris.

India was much quieter when I was a child, far more formal and closed. Women rarely worked. Everyone went to bed early, social life was strictly structured and entirely associated with family, and nobody even went out to eat. The only way to have any feeling of freedom or experience of the bigger world was through books. My mother showed us how to escape and find space by reading and writing, even within the restrictions of life in the Indian middle class. We all read very intently. One of my deepest childhood memories is of summer afternoons spent lying outside with my mother and sister, reading. Time felt as if it completely stopped. We all expected those afternoons to go on for ever.

7 **Brooklyn** borough of New York city, west of Manhattan – 9 **loads** lots – 13 **strikingly** very noticeably – 20 **elaborate** *here:* highly decorated – 28 **intently** with great concentration

My mother's books appeared as if by magic. She kept her writing very private – we barely knew she was doing it, and we never knew what she was working on. I read most of the books when I was an adult. It was strange to discover that our loving, tender mother had also been a different person all along. I was completely unconscious as a child of how hard it was for her to produce her work. Her writing wasn't taken seriously by anyone around, and I have only realised the strength it must have taken her to carry on since becoming an adult. I'm sure I would not have managed that degree of discipline myself.

I wasn't aware of why my parents separated; nor did I question it. When I went to Cambridge with my mother, we experienced being immigrants together – learning how to get a phone and car, and getting used to a very unfamiliar way of socialising. It must have been hard for her, in her late forties, to get a job for the first time, to work, teach and negotiate a new country. But I never had a clue about all the worry and the terror she must have experienced.

It was hard for me at the age of 14 to leave my familiar home and go to such a different, fast-paced country on the other side of the world. It still feels strange today in a way. When I go back to see my father in India, I envy how comfortable, happy and unselfconscious he is in his environment. We aren't like that, my mother and I. We wouldn't want to go back; but it's very difficult, once you begin to travel, to stop.

As soon as I enter my mother's house, I can read and write and think in a completely different way, and I feel so happy. Ideas come into my head. She is such a calm presence. There's no drama or misery. She isn't aggressive or competitive. She never had that monstrous ego some writers develop; she brings space with her, rather than squeezing everybody else out with her personality. She takes that feeling with her no matter where she is.

5 **tender** kind – 16 **to negotiate** *here:* to find one's way around – 17 **never had a clue** had no idea – 20 **fast-paced** hectic – 23 **unselfconscious** natural, not trying to play a role

We'll have breakfast together and read all the papers, then we write in different rooms. We meet for lunch, then in the afternoon we usually run errands, read and write more, and always have a very happy time cooking dinner together. Reading and writing is at the centre of both our lives and our relationship with each other. All our talk is about books, writers and reading, although never about what we're actually working on at the moment. I spend years knowing nothing about what she is writing until I see the finished product.

I wish I could stay with her and work all the time. I talk to her every day on the phone when I'm not with her. It would be very difficult to write without her around. I can't bear the thought of her growing old. It is the greatest terror of my life.

Interviews by Katharine Hibbert in *The Sunday Times*, September 23, 2007.

3 **to run errands** to do various little jobs

3. A Letter to the Editor

To
The Editor,
Times of India

Dear Sir,

This is in reference to an article in the *Sunday Times of India*, dated 19th September 1999, titled "An accidental Parsi" (page no.4). The article was in very bad taste. It includes various false, baseless and unwarranted allegations on the Zoroastrian community. It has hurt the feelings of every true and faithful Zoroastrian (unlike Ms. Meher Pestonji). It is senseless and derogatory. [...]

I would like to put forth some of my arguments on some of these points and clear some misconceptions in the mind of this "accidental Parsi".

1) Ms. Meher Pestonji says, and I quote, "After my divorce, I became a freelance journalist and came into contact with a different set of attitudes, contrary to those of my childhood friends. There was this split in my thinking, my identity. Being a journalist and a Parsi are two separate things, and often these clashed. My perception as a journalist prevailed over any kind of loyalty to my community – which I don't have." [...]

The Zoroastrian religion preaches righteousness (Asha), purity (spiritual and physical), truthfulness [...]. A Zoroastrian is

6 **accidental** *here:* by chance or coincidence – 6 **Parsi** member the Zoroastrian community in India, descendant of those who emigrated from Persia after the 7th century Islamic conquest – 8 **unwarranted** not needed or appropriate – 8 **allegation** unproved statement, accusation – 8 **Zoroastrian** follower of Zoroaster (c. 628–551 B.C.), a Persian prophet also called Zarathustra – 10 **Meher Pestonji** see pp. 19–20 – 11 **derogatory** insulting – 13 **misconception** misunderstanding, mistake – 16 **freelance** not paid a salary, working on a free basis – 17 **contrary to** in opposition to, very different from – 20 **to clash** to be in conflict – 20 **perception** *here:* way of seeing things – 20 **to prevail** to dominate – 22 **to preach** to teach (morality) – 22 **righteousness** correct behaviour

required to be truthful, straightforward, and to fight against evil. (These requirements are a must for every good human being).

I suppose, and you will definitely agree that these qualities of truthfulness, straightforwardness are also very important for a journalist [...]. So I fail to understand, that in the case of Ms. Meher Pestonji, she faces these clashes of identity.

As you must be aware Zoroastrians were the pioneers of journalism in India. Mr. Fardunji Marzbanji founded the first newspaper in India and the sixteenth oldest in the world [...]. Since then the community has produced many famous journalists. They were devout Zoroastrians, but their identities never clashed.

2) Ms. Meher Pestonji says, and I quote, “The Parsis were pampered by the British and haven’t really adjusted as a community (as opposed to individual or corporate excellence) in the post-British period. Parsis are westernised – and value that. My main grouse against the community is that it has not assimilated into the mainstream.” [...]

Our community has produced many stalwarts such as Sir Jamsetji Jeejeebhoy, (the most benevolent philantrophist), Mr. Pherozeshah Mehta (the father of the Bombay Municipal Corporation), Mr. Dadabhoy Naoroji (first Indian to be a member of the British Parliament), Sir. Cowasjee Jehangir, Mr. Dinshaw Vaccha, Mr. Khurshed Nariman (Veer Nariman), etc.. The list could go on. No doubt that the British were in awe of the contribution of this microscopic community and respected it.

Members of our community are found in all spheres of daily life and we have become part of the mainstream, however we try and maintain our own distinct identity. [...]

3) Ms. Meher Pestonji says, and I quote, “The fact that we are still building housing colonies exclusively for Parsis in this day

1 **evil** badness, wickedness (*das Böse*) – 11 **devout** [dɪˈvaʊt] faithful, taking one’s religion seriously – 13 **to pamper** to treat in an over-friendly way, to spoil – 13 **to adjust** to adapt – 14 **corporate** of an organized group – 16 **grouse** (*inf*) complaint – 18 **stalwart** [ˈstɔːlwət] strong representative – 19 **benevolent** [bɪˈnevələnt] kindly, showing good will – 24 **in awe of** full of admiration for – 28 **to maintain** to keep up

and age speaks for itself. This feeling that we are apart from the rest is a very questionable way of thinking." [...]

Our forefathers were foresighted enough to provide the basic infrastructural facilities for our community. It was done to protect the interests of our community. Had it not been for them so many of our economically weaker brothers and sisters would have remained homeless. There is nothing wrong when the community leaders protect the interests of the community.

4) Ms. Meher Pestonji says, and I quote, "Why is Parsi charity limited only to their kind? How can they be so insensitive to the poorest of the poor? Very little Parsi charity reaches the ordinary pavementwallah, streetkid or slumdweller. But then their own poor are nowhere near the poorest of non-Parsis. Parsis proudly call themselves philanthropic but the reality is something else." [...]

It is a completely false statement that Parsi charity is limited only for Parsis. Take for instance the Sir J.J. Hospital at Byculla, Mumbai. It is a very fine example of how the Parsi charity has reached the poorest of the poor. Parsi schools such as the Sir J.J. School, the Byramjee Jeejeebhoy Parsi Charitable Institution (school & junior college), the Cowasjee Jehangir School, the Jehangir Burjorji Vaccha school, etc. [...] Their students are not just restricted to Zoroastrian children, even non-Zoroastrian children are admitted. In fact the number of non-Zoroastrian children in these schools far exceed the number of Zoroastrian children.

I would therefore request you to retrospect your decision of having allowed the printing of such a senseless article in your esteemed newspaper. [...]

From

Mr. B. V.

3 **foresighted** with a clear vision of the future – 12 **pavementwallah** (*partly Hindi*) person working on the streets – 17 **Mumbai** new official name of Bombay – 23 **to admit** to allow to attend – 24 **to exceed** to be greater in number – 28 **esteemed** with a high reputation

4. *East, West* – a Review

In his first major work of fiction since *The Satanic Verses*, Salman Rushdie gives us nine short stories steeped in fantasy, memory, history and fable. This should come as no surprise. In part, these tales continue the stylistic approach the author has used since his early novel *Midnight's Children*. But more to the point, a retreat into memory and fantasy seems a logical response to living in seclusion under the threat of death.

East, West (Pantheon, 214 pp), a strong collection on the whole, is divided into three symmetrical sections. The best of these sections is the last, also titled "East, West," where diverse cultures collide. The three tales included here, which all derive from the memories of their narrators, show Rushdie's keen eye for telling details, playful verbal imagination and sharp sense of humor. In "The Courter," a man remembers his boyhood in a London apartment, relating the love affair between the building's courtly Indian porter and a tiny, 60-year-old Indian woman [...]. In the quietly told and moving "The Harmony of the Spheres," a native Indian living in England remembers his longtime relationship with a close friend, a British writer afflicted with paranoid schizophrenia who commits suicide. "Chekov and Zulu," the third tale in this section, follows two boyhood friends from India whose love for *Star Trek* becomes their secret code as they navigate careers as diplomats (and sometime spies) in Britain.

The collection's fine opening section, "East," contains three stripped-down tales that resonate like fables. In each, the characters' misguided or deceitful actions lead to their moral comeuppance. "Good Advice is Rarer than Rubies," for example,

1 **Salman Rushdie** see p. 40 – 2 **steeped in** full of, as if immersed in (*usu* a liquid) – 6 **retreat** backward movement – 7 **in seclusion** alone – 11 **to derive from** to come, take meaning from – 13 **telling** *here:* significant – 16 **courtly** with formal, old-fashioned manners – 20 **schizophrenia** [ˌskɪtsəʊˈfriːnɪə] a psychotic condition that causes hallucinations – 22 **Star Trek** long-running TV science fiction series (*Raumschiff Enterprise*) – 23 **to navigate** to find one's way through (*here fig*) – 26 **stripped down** *here:* reduced to a minimum – 26 **to resonate** to send back sound or vibrations (*here fig*) – 28 **comeuppance** (*inf*) satisfying defeat (*usu* of an arrogant or unsympathetic person)

tells of a man who preys on the vulnerable women who come to the British consulate seeking visas to England. He meets his match in a feisty, beautiful young Pakistani woman who ends up keeping her wallet while stealing his heart. "The Free Radio" chronicles a handsome young rickshaw driver who dreams of becoming a Bombay movie star, but marries the widow of the town thief, a woman with five children who convinces him to undergo a government-sponsored vasectomy. In "The Prophet's Hair," an amateur collector's failure to return a stolen national treasure – a single hair from the Prophet Mohammed, encased in a glass vial and taken from Hazratbal mosque – leads to the ruination of his family.

The section titled "West" is the book's weakest. Particularly baffling is the glib and unengaging "At the Auction of the Ruby Slippers." Set in a vaguely defined post-apocalyptic world where everyone seems to be dying of an unnamed disease, the story concerns the auctioning off of a highly prized pair of red slippers – presumably those worn by the character Dorothy in *The Wizard of Oz*. If only the author could click his heels together and make this weak piece disappear. Rushdie redeems himself in comic "Christopher Columbus & Queen Isabella of Spain Consummate Their Relationship." Here we see Columbus, an ambitious sycophant groveling for ships and supplies, humiliated by a queen who taunts and denies him for the mere sport of it. But not to worry, for Columbus triumphs in the end and sets off to discover America.

All told, Rushdie has produced in his first short-story collection a lively, smart and pleasing book. Most of the stories in *East, West* leave one wishing for more. While this fact speaks well

1 **to prey on** to make a victim of in order to gain some advantage – 1 **vulnerable** easy to hurt or take advantage of – 3 **his match** *(inf)* his equal – 3 **feisty** strong and confident – 4 **wallet** ['wɒlɪt] purse – 5 **to chronicle** to tell the story of – 8 **vasectomy** operation to make a man infertile – 11 **vial** ['vaɪəl] thin glass container – 13 **baffling** puzzling – 14 **glib** fluent but insincere – 14 **unengaging** not exciting one's interest – 18 **The Wizard of Oz** famous Hollywood film (1939), based on a children's story by Frank L. Baum – 20 **to redeem os** *here:* to regain the reader's favour – 22 **sycophant** *(inf)* ['sɪkəfənt] sb who pretends admiration or respect in order to gain some advantage – 23 **to grovel** ['grɒvl] to bend down humbly before sb – 23 **to humiliate** to destroy sb's dignity – 24 **to taunt** to mock and try to provoke

of his talent, it also perhaps is a sign that he is really a novelist at heart. Based on what he has given here in short fables and snatches of memory, one looks forward to the next major project he chooses to undertake.

Article by Mark Bautz in *Insight on the News*, March 13, 1995 (abridged).

3 **snatch** *here:* small piece

5. A Declaration of Independence

She'd lived her entire childhood by the rules. Then, one day, Bharati Mukherjee slid into the driver's seat ... Here she describes that decisive childhood incident for American talk show host Oprah Winfrey:

As a bookish child in Calcutta, I used to thrill to the adventures of bad girls whose pursuit of happiness swept them outside the bounds of social decency. Tess of the d'Urbervilles, Emma Bovary and Anna Karenina lived large in my imagination. The naughty girls of Hollywood films flirted and knew how to drive. These reckless women felt more real to me than the unselfish relatives I was expected to emulate. Growing up in an old-fashioned Bengali Hindu family and going to a convent school run by stern Irish nuns, I was brought up to revere rules. Without rules, there was only anarchy.

My mother's rules had to do with feminine deportment, so I never played hard enough to break a toy or muddy my dress. My father's rules had to do with never shaming the family by even a hint of scandal, and not providing business rivals with an opportunity to kidnap me or throw acid in my face. (There are real consequences to disobedience.) Good behavior meant not falling in love until my father found the right bridegroom and never protesting his decrees. Kidnap-proofing meant never traveling to and from school in a car without a driver, two armed guards and my watchful mother.

2 **Bharati Mukherjee** see pp. 59–60 – 4 **Oprah Winfrey** (b. 1954) host of highest-rating US talk show, with very influential book club – 5 **bookish** fond of reading – 6 **pursuit** attempt to reach or achieve (*v.* to pursue); phrase used in American Declaration of Independence, 1776 – 7 **decency** good moral behaviour – 7 **Tess of the d'Urbervilles** heroine of the English novel (1891) of that title; by Thomas Hardy – 7 **Emma Bovary** heroine of the French novel (1957) of that title; by Gustave Flaubert – 8 **Anna Karenina** heroine of the Russian novel (1877) of that title; by Leo Tolstoy – 9 **naughty** (esp. of children) badly-behaved – 10 **reckless** careless of danger – 11 **to emulate** to copy, take as a model of behaviour – 12 **Bengali** of the state of Bengal, in eastern India – 12 **Hindu** polytheistic religion, dominant in India – 13 **stern** strict – 13 **to revere** to have great respect for – 15 **deportment** proper way of carrying os, standing, walking, etc. – 16 **to muddy** to make dirty with mud from the ground – 19 **to kidnap** to capture in order to demand money for release – 21 **bridegroom** husband-to-be – 22 **decree** authoratitative ruling – 22 **proofing** making secure from

Not, not, not. Never, never, never.

One day, as I was being driven home from the university, our driver asked me – I'll never know why – if I wanted to learn to drive. To be a young woman in India in the 1950s and to drive a car was to be Anna and Emma – even Doris Day. I slipped behind the Rover's steering wheel. Within seconds, we were edging toward a ring of squatters. The car kept drifting; I screamed; the chauffeur shouted and pulled the brake. I didn't hit anyone, but for the first time I found myself in a situation that my entire upbringing had aimed to prevent. In India, there are real consequences to inattention; drivers who jeopardize pedestrians can be lynched on the spot. I scrambled for the backseat. The chauffeur bundled one wailing squatter into the car and sped home. My father took charge. Presumably, a few – maybe many – rupees changed hands. The driver was reprimanded and shortly thereafter sent back to Calcutta. I never admitted my misdeed.

In the events of that day lies the germ of a destiny far less certain than my father had intended. Acting on instinct, I had challenged my upbringing. I'd seen the last demonstration of his protective power. I might have failed my first unchaperoned probing of the adult world, but within a year, my sisters and I would be living on our own in America, a place he'd never seen. We would all make love matches, defying his choice of suitable grooms.

5 **Doris Day** American actress and singer; starred in many popular romantic comedies of the 1950s and 60s – 6 **Rover** British make of car – 7 **to edge toward** *(mainly AE)* to move gradually nearer – 7 **squatter** ['skwɒtə] sb who occupies land or a house in order to claim a right to live there – 10 **upbringing** family training – 11 **to jeopardize** ['dʒepədaɪz] to endanger – 12 **to lynch** to kill in revenge, without waiting for legal action – 13 **to bundle** *here:* to push or pull – 13 **to wail** to cry loudly and continuously – 15 **rupee** Indian currency unit – 16 **to reprimand** to formally criticize or blame – 18 **germ** *here:* small beginning of sth – 18 **destiny** fate, what has to happen – 21 **unchaperoned** (*usu* of a young girl or couple) not supervised – 22 **to probe** to test – 24 **love match** marriage for love (i.e. not arranged) – 24 **to defy** to go against or resist (authority)

The transgression was small, unconfessed and unforgiven. My long-suppressed inner bad girl had spoken. “Drive,” she said. “Take a risk, be cunning, lie.” She might even have said: “Write.”

Article by Bharati Mukherjee in *O, The Oprah Magazine*, August 2002.

1 **transgression** breaking of a rule; sin or crime – 1 **unconfessed** not openly admitted – 2 **to suppress** to keep under control – 3 **cunning** clever and calculating

Useful Phrases for Discussing the Short Stories

/ indicates a synonym
, indicates that the following word can also be used with the verb

The story

to be concerned with the theme of ...
to deal with .../to be about .../to focus on .../to revolve around ...
the story is set in .../takes place in ...
to be subdivided into ... parts/sections
to constitute the turning-point
to reach the climax
the story develops/progresses/unfolds ...

The narrator

to be told by an omniscient, first-person, third-person narrator
to be an impartial observer
to be told in a neutral/factual/unbiased way
to give an insight into the character's frame of mind
to tell the story from one character's perspective/point of view
to have a limited, unlimited point of view
to create a gloomy/dejected atmosphere/... an atmosphere of decay, aggressiveness

Stylistic devices

to make use of *(name of a stylistic device)* ... in order to ...
to serve as/to function as a structuring device
to be a recurring motif
to represent/stand for/to be a symbol of/to be a sign of/to signify/to express ...
the metaphorical/symbolic use of ... indicates ...

the imagery of … has a whole/wide range of functions
the theme of … finds a corresponding image in …
to illustrate/to throw light on …
to serve as the key to …
to underline the crucial importance of …
to foreshadow sth
to connote/to imply/to suggest
to allude to/to hint at/to refer to
to have a tragic, happy, satisfactory, open ending
to be told in flashbacks
to serve as a setting for …

The character

to present the protagonist as sb who …
to be a round character
to be a flat/one-dimensional character
to perceive sb as being …
to come across as being …
sb can be described as …/can be characterized as being …
sb is characterized by the way he or she speaks, looks etc.
to present oneself as being …
to be presented as sb who …/introduced as sb who … depicted as sb who …/shown to be, have, etc. …/ portrayed as sb who …
to be a person of (great, little) …
one of his/her main characteristics/traits is …
to show a disposition towards doing sth
to have a (strong) inclination/tendency to do sth
this trait is best exemplified/shown/depicted/illustrated in the passage where …
to characterize sb directly/indirectly

Relationships

to be antagonists
to be unable/to find it difficult to relate to sb
to interact with the natives/indigenous population (on equal, unequal terms; well)
to go native (= to adopt the native way of life)
to be cut off from society
to be dependent on sb
to display a favourable/sympathetic, arrogant, resentful, scornful, contemptuous, mistrustful attitude towards sb
to behave in a superior, condescending, patronizing, derisive, hostile way towards sb
to respond to sb in a caring, benevolent, understanding way
to treat sb as an inferior, an equal, a subordinate
to regard sb as a figure of authority
the relationship worsens/deteriorates, breaks down/fails
to improve/strengthen, maintain, form, discontinue a relationship
to suffer ill-treatment at the hands of sb
to have to put up with unfair, inhumane, degrading, harsh treatment
to be victimized
to be alienated/to be estranged from one's culture, one's surroundings
to assume, gain, achieve, assert, exert dominance over sb
to challenge, undermine, call into question sb's/a culture's/a superior's power, authority
to experience isolation, loneliness
to feel detached from sth

Acknowledgements

Anita Desai, *A Devoted Son* from *Games at Twilight and other Stories.* Copyright © 1978 Anita Desai. Reproduced by permission of the author c/o Rogers, Coleridge & White Ltd., 20 Powis Mews, London W11 1JN.

Meher Pestonji, *Outsider.* Copyright © Meher Pestonji. Reprinted with permission of the author.

Salman Rushdie, *Good Advice is Rarer than Rubies* and *The Free Radio.* Copyright © 1994 Salman Rushdie. Reprinted by permission of the Wylie Agency (UK) Ltd. All rights reserved.

Bharati Mukherjee, *Nostalgia.* Copyright © 1985 by Bharai Mukherjee. Originally published in *Darkness.* Reprinted with permission of the author.

Additional Materials:

Katherine Hibbert, *Relative Values: Anita Desai and her Daughter Kiran.* Copyright © 2007 NI Syndication, London.

Nicht in allen Fällen war es uns möglich, den Rechteinhaber ausfindig zu machen. Berechtigte Ansprüche werden selbstverständlich im Rahmen der branchenüblichen Vereinbarungen abgegolten.

Picture credits

p. 5: Corbis (McPherson), Düsseldorf;
p. 19: Meher Pestonji, Bombay, Apollo Reclamation;
p. 41: ullstein bild (AP), Berlin
p. 59: Bharati Mukherjee, EMMA DODGE HANSON